Practical Pre-School Books

D1685818

Faiths and festivals Book 2:
A month-by-month guide to multicultural celebrations around the year

Leeds City College
Beeston Centre

Published by Practical Pre-School Books, A Division of MA Education Ltd, St Jude's Church, Dulwich Road, Herne Hill, London, SE24 0PB.

Tel: 020 7738 5454

www.practicalpreschoolbooks.com

© MA Education Ltd 2013

Design: Alison Cutler fonthillcreative 01722 717043

All images © MA Education Ltd.

All photos taken by Lucie Carlier with the exception of front cover, main image © Julia Mashkova/Fotolia, side panel (top to bottom) © iStockphoto.com/Eileen Hart,

© iStockphoto.com/HAIBO BI, © iStockphoto.com/Christine Keene; page 17 © iStockphoto.com/jabaa; page 20 © SXC/TALUDA; page 34 © Karen Hart; page 39 © iStockphoto.com/flytosky11; page 49 © iStockphoto.com/DistinctiveImages; page 50 © iStockphoto.com/pictafolio; page 53 © iStockphoto.com/AtomicSparkle; page 65 © iStockphoto.com/pelvidge.

ISBN 978-1-907241-43-7

25824

Introduction

Exploring our world

Celebrating faiths and festivals is a great way of introducing young children to new cultures and religions. By gaining a knowledge and respect of other's identities, customs and beliefs, we learn to appreciate both the diversities and similarities among all human beings and – what an interesting subject to work with – the way people all over the world come together to celebrate, give thanks and have fun!

How to use this book

This book was designed as a resource for anyone working with pre-school children wishing to incorporate world religions and celebrations into their planning.

The first chapter covers learning and teaching RE; requirements and methods. The main section of the book covers festivals and celebrations as they occur throughout the year, with a chapter for each calendar month. These include activity resources such as recipes or scripts. Festivals include those most commonly celebrated, but also some of those less well-known, but which lend themselves particularly well to pre-school activities. A background section on religious places and practices is also included at the back of the book, along with setting examples for further inspiration.

The month-by-month calendar page opposite can be used for recording special events planned for your own setting, or any planned events in your local area, which you feel may be of interest to families in your group. This page can also be copied and given to families, or enlarged and displayed on the wall at your setting!

The book is an ideal companion to *Faiths and Festivals 1* by Christine Howard et al., also available from Practical Pre-School Books.

Month-by-month calendar

JANUARY	FEBRUARY	MARCH
APRIL	MAY	JUNE
JULY	AUGUST	SEPTEMBER
OCTOBER	NOVEMBER	DECEMBER

Faiths and festivals Book 2: A month-by-month guide to multicultural celebrations around the year

www.practicalpreschoolbooks.com

Teaching world faiths and cultures

Aims and principles

Whilst devising this book, I reflected on the points I consider to be the fundamental principles when teaching world faiths and cultures to early years children.

The following points are my thoughts on important goals.

All settings should aim to enrich each individual child's life through positive experience by:

- Aiming to instil a sense of self-worth in all children

- Aiming to enrich the lives of children by encouraging companionship with all

- Aiming to encourage children to express personal preferences, feelings and needs, whilst appreciating those of others

- Valuing and cherishing all children for the person they are, irrespective of, and acknowledged for, their individual cultural, social, and racial background

- Children consistently feeling a valued member of their pre-school group

- Involving families wherever you can – never being afraid to ask parents to help clarify your cultural or religious queries.

What we must teach

The Education Reform Act 1988

The Education Reform Act 1988 states that every local authority should have an agreed syllabus, locally determined, which must 'reflect the fact that the religious traditions in Great Britain are in the main Christian, whilst taking account of the teaching and practices of other principal religions represented in Great Britain'. The need for a more multi-cultural view of RE was again considered in the Education Act 1996, making religious education part of the curriculum for all children in schools.

Today, children in England and Wales have the right to receive religious education of an informative nature, reflecting our multi-cultural society and diverse religious beliefs. The requirements in Scotland are a bit different, with RE incorporated into RME (religious and moral education) for the 5-14 years curriculum, with Northern Ireland just beginning to use a multi-faith curriculum for the teaching of RE.

An agreed syllabus

Unlike subjects covered in the National Curriculum, the teaching of religious education is taught within guidelines produced by each individual local authority. This 'agreed syllabus' is devised by representatives of main religious faiths in that community, consisting of teachers, local authority officers and representatives of the Church of England. They may also include guidance on the teaching of RE in early years.

The Early Years Foundation Stage (EYFS)

The foundation stage focuses on the needs of children from birth to age five and through to Reception. There is a legal obligation to provide religious education to reception class children, but not to nursery. However, the 2012 EYFS statutory framework for teaching requires early years educators should be covering the following points – which will be covered by the activities in each chapter of the book, as well as many additional aspects of learning connected to other areas of learning development:

Personal, Social and Emotional Development: Aspects of Learning

- Making Relationships

- Self-confidence and Self-awareness

- Managing feelings and behaviour.

Understanding the World: Aspects of Learning

- People and Communities

- The World

- Technology.

Expressive Arts and Design: Aspects of Learning

- Exploring and using media and materials

- Being imaginative.

Enhancing your provision

Building on community and identity

Each and every child arriving at your setting arrives as a ready-made package of cultural experience – so why waste it? See if you can get families to supply some photos of family members and their homes for display in your setting; especially beneficial at the start of the settling in process, as children then feel they are spending time in a place they already belong. Take time to get to know family members, finding out when cultural events are to be celebrated and talking to individual children about these experiences.

Try to create an environment where familiarity and identity play important parts in children's lives – organise a 'foods of the world' day, sending letters home to parents asking for contributions of favourite cultural foods for children to sample, welcome parents into your setting to share favourite stories, songs and rhymes, have cultural ornaments and pictures displayed in your setting, and make the sharing of news an important part of the day, thus keeping children within the group the focus of that learning. Set lots of time aside for circle time sessions – great opportunities for bringing everyone together and sharing news.

When assessing strengths and weaknesses in your setting, be sure to include the area of welcoming children and their families. You could send a simple questionnaire home asking if parents felt fully welcomed and for any suggestions on ways to further family involvement.

Learning as a positive experience

When it comes to the teaching of religion, practitioners can feel they're entering a contentious area of education. We hear many stories in the popular press of parents taking children out of school because of a policy at odds with their beliefs, or of children being excluded from lessons for wearing non-uniform religious dress, for example, and these stories give the impression that you need to be wary when touching on the subject of faith. Although it is true that some parents may have reservations concerning their children learning about

religions other than their own, if you do find parents have such concerns, it is important to explain that you only intend to mark religious festivals, and not promote their philosophy.

Building connections with the wider community

Organising outings is a lovely way of introducing children to new people and situations and can be kept inexpensive and simple by using your local area. Try going on a group walk around a local shopping area and talking about all the people and different types of shops you see, both along the way, and once back at your setting, also, ask around to see if any local businesses are willing to let your children come in, have a look and ask questions. This type of activity is a great way of introducing new people and experiences, having a look around a Chinese or Indian restaurant for example, may well be a new experience for many children and there's sure to be lots of cultural decoration on display to point out and talk about.

It is when we learn about other people's lives that we build connections with others, discovering that as different as one person's beliefs may be from another ultimately, it has nothing to do with the building of friendships, and once we start to look beyond the familiar, we find there are lots of new friends just waiting to be made, and we truly become part of the wider community.

The purpose of dramatic play in early years – why use drama?

As a drama teacher, I have used the subject of world festivals, cultures and customs many times during pre-school drama classes, on several occasions developing work starting life as little role play improvisations into simple performance pieces – many of which are included in this book.

Almost all young children naturally engage with role play scenarios through ordinary play, naturally taking on identities and playing out new situations. This important element of play helps children make sense of what they see going on around them, giving them perspective, helping them engage with their environment and culture and acting as a sharing of both individual and joint experiences. This is especially important for children from minority faiths and cultures, possibly with English as a second language, who may, through finding it difficult to communicate with others, find themselves somewhat isolated from informal group play, but can be brought together with other children in little role play activities – making friends.

Using drama in pre-school settings encourages:

● Language skills

- Integration – social interaction

- Inspiration and motivation to further learning

- Creativity and imagination.

Storytelling and storymaking

Stories are the backbone of drama and all creative thinking. For many, storytelling sessions represent very happy childhood memories, with the stories told – either read or made-up by our parents and carers, often remembered and re-told to new generations of children for years to come. Try not to think of storytelling as something used to fill a gap at the end of circle time, but as an important part of the day. Plan for your storytimes and make them work for you – using stories to underpin learning in all areas of early years education.

Using stories is a great way of sharing knowledge, even as adults, we remember facts much more efficiently when learnt in this way, taking on real meaning when put into context through a story.

In this book I have used, where possible, the traditional stories associated with individual festivals, to illustrate, demonstrate and consolidate their meaning. I have also used rhymes and contemporary role-play scenarios where appropriate, to aid learning and to have fun! It's not all drama!

There are lots of different types of activities to try in this book, as well as the role play/improvisation and storytelling activities.

I have included special festival foods to make and try, craft activities, games to play, costumes to make, circle time fun and lots more.

The activities in this book have been designed to be:

- **Suitable for participation at all levels of ability**

- **Low on resources**

- **In line with the EYFS Development Matters framework**

- **Fun.**

Issues to consider: Special Educational Needs (SEN) provision

Children are said to have a special educational need if they have a learning difficulty, which calls for special educational provision to be made for them.

As early years practitioners, the extent/type of involvement with children with SEN will differ greatly in each provision. Addressing a child's special needs at pre-school level is massively important, as these early years are a crucial time in a child's development and identifying any problems early on can be vital to the extent of progress gained both in early years and later life.

Young children learn through being with others and sharing experiences of the world around them – and they all learn at their own pace. However, some children will show clear signs of falling behind other children of their age.

Signs of learning delay will often show themselves in the following areas:

- Communication

- Understanding and learning

- Sensory and physical development

- Behaviour or relating to other people.

January: New Year traditions around the world

Why is New Year celebrated?

Although there are wide variations in the way New Year is celebrated throughout the world – even when it is celebrated, there is one unifying thread that ties all celebrations together, the sense of renewed opportunity, of this being a time to forgive old grievances – a chance to start afresh.

The following activities represent a kind of pick-and-mix selection of cultural New Year celebrations. I chose the countries represented because their celebrations are unusual and fun. The idea is to show that while New Year is a time of celebration the world over, it is celebrated in many different ways.

Hogmanay – Scottish New Year

There's no doubt that the Scottish people know how to celebrate New Year with a passion – famously loving a good party!

Many Scots still honour some of their ancient traditions to this day, with one of their oldest customs still widely held throughout the country being that of **'First Footing'**. Shortly after the stroke of midnight, neighbours visit each other's houses to wish a Happy New Year. Members of each household wait to see who will be the first person to cross their doorway, hopefully a tall, dark haired young man, as he will traditionally bring the best luck – thought to be a throwback to Viking days when fair haired

Recipe for easy-to-make Scottish shortbread

A simple, traditional recipe to make with young children as an example of a food traditionally made and eaten in Scotland as part of the New Year celebrations.

Makes about 16 pieces

Preparation time: 20 minutes

Cooking time: 20-25 minutes

Ingredients:

- 225g butter

- 110g fine caster sugar, plus extra for sprinkling

- 225g plain flour, plus extra for dusting work surface

- 100g cornflour

- Pinch of salt.

Method:

Preheat oven to 325°F/170°C Gas Mark 3.

In a large bowl cream together the butter, sugar and little pinch of salt until light, fluffy and pale in colour. This can take a little time so alternatively, use a food mixer.

Mix flour and cornflour together and sieve into the bowl, mixing all ingredients together thoroughly, but without over-mixing.

Knead lightly on a floured surface to form a loose dough, then roll to approximately 1cm thick.

Cut out shapes with cookie cutters, gently pricking the top of biscuits with a fork.

Place on a lightly greased baking sheet and bake for 20-25 minutes or until firm and golden.

Sprinkle with caster sugar while still warm.

Leave to cool on a wire rack.

strangers arriving on your doorstep meant big trouble. This first footer should come bearing symbolic gifts such as coal, bread, a coin, salt, black bun (type of fruit cake), shortbread and whisky as symbols of life, prosperity, food, warmth and good cheer. These days usually just the shortbread and whisky are given – and most welcomed!

Auld Lang Syne

One of Britain's most well-known traditional songs, 'Auld Lang Syne', translated into English as 'Long, Long Ago', is traditionally sung as the clock strikes twelve on New Year's Eve to welcome in the new year, and comes from a poem by famous Scottish poet, Robert Burns. 'Auld Lang Syne' is well known throughout the world, especially in English speaking countries and is sometimes also sung at funerals, graduations and other occasions marking an ending or farewell of some kind.

Activity ideas

- Bring in samples of some of the gifts a 'First Footer' might bring on New Years Day, explaining what they are during a circle-time session. Many children will have no knowledge of coal or where it comes from, or how we come to have salt, so this could be used as a nice starting point for a group conversation on the subject of where things come from.

- Help children make some traditional **Scottish shortbread** for a snack-time treat (see simple recipe on page 9).

- On New Years Day, Scottish children get up nice and early and visit neighbours houses singing songs for which they are given little treats such as: mince pies, apples, sweets or coins – a bit like carol singing. The singing must be over by noon or the singers are called fools. For a change from your usual circle time songs, have a go at the following traditional Scottish children's rhymes which have all been in circulation for many years in both the homes and playgrounds of Scotland.

- See if you can find a recording of 'Auld Lang Syne' for children to listen to, before getting everyone standing in a circle, arms linked in the traditional way, to show the traditional Scottish custom.

Dan Dan the funny wee man

Dan Dan the funny wee man
washed his face in the frying pan
combed his hair with the leg of a chair
Dan Dan the funny wee man

Dance to your daddy

Dance to your daddy,
My bonnie laddie,
Dance to your daddy, my bonnie lamb!

And you'll get a fishy, on a little dishy
And you'll get a fishy, when the boat comes home.

Dance to your daddy,
My bonnie laddie,
Dance to your daddy, my bonnie lamb!

Talk about Scottish dialect, explaining the following words:

- Wee – Little

- Bonnie – Beautiful or handsome

- Bairn – Child or baby

- Laddie – Boy

- Lass or lassie – Girl

- Stooshie – A big fuss or row

- Wean – Child (mainly used in the west of Scotland, derived from wee-one or little-one)

- Glaikit – Silly

- Braw – Pretty or pleasant.

Russian New Year

For Russian people, New Year is the biggest celebration of the year, and is steeped in lovely traditions and customs. The most important figures at New Year are **Father Frost** and his fairy granddaughter **Snegurochka**, or **Snow Maiden**. Their arrival is eagerly anticipated by children all over Russia, as they are the Russian equivalent of Santa Claus and his helpful Christmas elf. Father Frost traditionally wears a long

Russian teacakes

Makes about 36 teacakes

Preparation time: 20 minutes

Cooking time: 12 minutes

Ingredients:

- 22g butter

- 5ml vanilla extract

- 50g icing sugar – plus extra 40g for rolling

- 250g plain flour.

Method:

Preheat oven to 350°F/180°C Gas Mark 4.

Cream butter and vanilla together until smooth.

Stir in 6 tablespoons of icing sugar and the flour until just blended.

Roll dough into 1 inch balls, placing them 2 inches apart on an ungreased baking sheet.

Bake for 12 minutes. When cool, roll teacakes in the remaining icing sugar.

Serve as a snack time treat.

red coat just like Santa, but in recent years he is sometimes represented as wearing blue or white, being colours associated with frost and, unlike secretive Santa, usually gives children gifts personally at New Year parties and celebrations. He also differs by using three horses to pull his sleigh in place of reindeer, has a long, waist length beard, in place of Santa's rather shorter version, carries a long, magical staff and is tall and athletic, where Santa is somewhat – cuddly! The Snow Maiden wears all white, with a crown of silver and pearls and is very beautiful.

Russian families celebrate the New Year by decorating their homes with a fir tree traditionally adorned with fruit, nuts, sweets and little wooden toys, but modern times have seen the addition of glass balls, tinsel and figures of Father Frost and the Snow Maiden.

Activity ideas

- All over Russia, in the early hours of News Years Day, fireworks fill the skies with light, adding to the party atmosphere of this special time. Bring this idea into your setting, by helping children make a lovely group, firework effects picture, using a large sheet of black paper and splatter painting bright colours using old toothbrushes as splatterers. Use lots of white to get a light, bright effect and keep clothes– and floor, well covered from flying paint. This makes a beautiful wall display for any setting.

- Another idea for a display poster is to have everyone helping to make a big collage of a fir tree. Simply draw the shape onto a large sheet of paper, then have children tear up scraps of green and brown paper to glue into place for the trunk and pine needles. Try collecting lots of old magazines in advance for this project, so children can help sort through the pages looking for brown and green sections – really good for encouraging colour recognition skills, this becomes a little activity on its own. You could choose specific children to help you sort colours, using children you feel could use some colour recognition practice. Once the fir tree is complete, write this English translation from part of the oldest of all traditional Russian rhymes underneath. It was written by a teacher over one hundred years ago and tells the story of a little fir tree, growing in the forest that comes to bring joy to children in their home.

The Little Fir Tree

In the forest a fir tree was born,
In the forest the fir tree grew,
In winter and summer she stands tall
And oh how green was she.

Thailand – Songkran Festival (Buddhist)

Thailand's most popular and widely celebrated festival, the Songkran Festival, begins on April 13th and lasts between three and ten days, depending on the region. The date, originally set by astrological calculation – the word Songkran deriving from the Sanskrit meaning for the beginning of a new solar year – is now fixed, and although Thailand now recognises the start of the new year as 1st January, the Songkran is celebrated more enthusiastically than ever before and has become quite a tourist attraction.

Although traditionally a time to visit and pay respect to elders, the most notable custom of Songkran today is the throwing of water – garden hoses, water guns or simple containers, they all come out at Songkran, and family, friends and passers-by all get a soaking – everyone's fair game!

Some people also make New Year resolutions during the Songkran Festival – to do more good things, being a popular pledge. Songkran is also thought of as a time for cleaning and renewal, with many Thais using this time to give their homes a good clean.

There is a more traditional side to the festival too and besides throwing water, people celebrating Songkran in a more traditional way – as a Buddhist festival, may visit a Wat (Buddhist monastery) to pray and offer food to the monks. It is also customary to wash any images of

Buddha, believing this will bring good luck and prosperity in the year ahead. In many Thai cities images of Buddha are paraded through the streets, giving people an opportunity to throw water over them as they pass by on decorated floats.

Fabulous Thai fruit salad

Try making a traditional Thai fruit salad – easy, healthy, and delicious too.

This activity is great for introducing young children to the idea of different fruits growing in other countries. Encourage children to have a little taste if they're initially reluctant to try, but if they still don't want to, leave it there – children get easily upset about trying new foods.

Choose from any of the listed traditional Thai fruits depending on what's in season. Try to use a mix of both familiar fruits and some which may be new to children in your group.

Mix some tinned fruits in with the fresh, using tinned pineapple and lychees for example – preparing these fresh is very sticky work. Cut grapes in half as they can easily get stuck in little throats, and make sure all chunks are cut nice and small to be on the safe side. Don't shy away from letting children have a go at cutting the fruit, use adult supervision, holding their fruit with a fork while they cut.

Place prepared fruits in individual bowls, letting children choose which fruits they'd like to put in their own bowl as a special snack time treat.

Some traditional Thai fruits:

- Banana
- Guava
- Watermelon
- Pineapple
- Orange
- Star fruit
- Papaya
- Mango
- Grapes
- Lychee.

Some questions to ask children while preparing and tasting fruit:

- How many different types of fruit can you name?
- Why are there stones and pips inside fruit?
- What are your favourite fruits?
- What does the outside/inside of the fruit look like?
- Does it smell nice?
- Do you think fruit is a healthy food?
- Why do you think some fruits only grow in other countries?

Have a toy-washing day

Pick a lovely sunny day for this one. Simply get some washing up bowls of soapy water, lots of little sponges and anything else you think might prove fun for water play, add any plastic dolls, cars etc., and let children give everything a good wash.

This simple activity is always a popular one, and a good activity to tie in with the Thai tradition of giving everything a good clean during Songkran.

Some spare clothes and towels might be a good idea though!

Group performance: New Year Celebrations everywhere!

A Thai boy squirting tourists with his water pistol, Danish children throwing old dishes at their neighbour's houses and children in Puerto Rico throwing pails of water out of their windows at midnight – It must be New Year! And, as welcoming the new year in with a celebration is one of the oldest, and probably most widely observed customs in the world – what better way to kick off the year than with a little celebration of your own?

This simple assembly style performance piece is perfect for sharing with parents and carers – and lots of fun too.

When organising any kind of performance with children this young, probably the most important thing to bear in mind is that it's never going to be a polished performance – and, that's the defining characteristic that will make it so special. Even if you manage to get things running just right before the event, once parents turn up there's a good chance everything you've practised will be forgotten, but, as anyone who has ever been to a child's performance will tell you – it is the bits the children make up on the spot that make it so special; the bits where they temporarily forget they are in a performance and run over to cuddle a little brother or sister…

Essential resources

- Triangles and beaters

- Little cake with a chocolate coin stuck in the top

- Small artificial Christmas tree placed on the floor or low table

- Sweets for the tree – candy canes or suitable small sweets tied with string and tree top star

- Water pistols – water optional

- Small bucket containing little pieces of torn paper

- Paper fans

- A few boxes wrapped in colourful paper – pretend presents

- Musical instrument box and/or hand-made shakers

- Xylophone

- …and a pair of red paper pants!

If you keep it all about fun, and treat performance activities as confidence building tasks focused on building social skills and friendships, the whole thing will be a success.

Things to do

- Gather together the **Essential resources** listed – making any changes to suit your own requirements along the way.

- Be sure to check out the **Make it!** section for instructions on making some of the (very simple) costume and prop pieces.

- Use the simple **script** (page 14) to narrate the stories of New Year celebrations in Greece, Spain, Thailand, Russia and Australia – following the performance instructions for children's parts.

Get everyone involved – have fun!

Make it!

Father Frost and Snow Girl hats

Keep things simple – all you really need here is a couple of woolly hats, a blue hat for father Frost and a white hat for Snow Girl.

Glue some cotton wool or fur fabric around the edge of each hat, and if you want to make them extra frosty looking, add some paper snowflakes sprinkled with glitter.

Russian New Year food plates

Make this a real fun activity, with children making their own special celebration plate of Russian New Year food.

Pre-draw the foods in the list below, giving each child a paper plate and a set of food pictures to colour-in, cut out and glue to their plate.

Typical Russian New Year food:

- Meat

- Peas/carrots/potatoes

- Pickles

- Onions

Script: Happy New Year around the world

Welcome to our special performance about the ways in which New Year is celebrated in five different countries – Greece, Spain, Thailand, Russia and Australia. We hope you find it interesting and maybe learn something new – And be warned, it could get rather noisy!

We begin in Greece; a beautiful country with hot summers, lots of islands and magnificent mountains, Greek children love New Year and celebrate by visiting neighbours houses, singing special Greek songs and playing triangles, which they play very fast and use to make a lot of noise – just like this;

(Children demonstrate playing their triangles as fast as they can)

If they are lucky, their neighbours will give them a few coins

(Child acting as a neighbour gives a few coins to the children with triangles)

In Greece children do not get presents on Christmas morning – they get them a week later on New Year's Day, when the special Greek Santa, called Saint Basil, visits good children. He looks just like the Santa we all know, dressed in red with a long white beard.

He is called St. Basil because many years ago there lived a very kind man named Basil, who spent much of his life helping poor people and those who wanted to learn about God. Because Greek people like to remember Basil's kindness on this special day, they named their Santa, St. Basil, and call New Year's Day – St. Basil's Day.

Families in Greece also sit down for a special St. Basil's Day meal together, and a special treat that is enjoyed by the whole family at New Year is a cake called a vasilopita. This cake has a coin or little gift baked inside and whoever finds the coin or gift in their slice of cake is said to be the lucky one – granted good luck all year long.

(A child sits on a chair with a little cake on a plate from which they pull a coin and happily hold it up for all to see – everyone else cheers hooray!)

In sunny Spain, New Year's Eve means one thing – Party Time! The Spanish people like to wear new red underwear on New Year's Eve because they believe this will bring them good luck in the year ahead.

(A child holds up the red pants for all to see)

Another funny thing that people in Spain like to do at New Year, is eat twelve grapes. People eat one grape each time the clock goes 'bong' for twelve o'clock midnight. The only trouble is, it is very difficult to buy seedless grapes in Spain, so most people accidently bite into the seeds which taste very sour – they end up pulling a silly face to welcome in the New Year.

(All children pretend to eat grapes and pull funny faces as teacher beats out twelve bongs on a xylophone)

People who live in a country called Thailand, celebrate New Year in April; the hottest time of the year in Thailand

(All children fan themselves with pre-made paper fans)

And the celebrations last for three days!

The people in Thailand call their New Year celebrations The Songkran Festival. During the Songkran Festival, people carry buckets of water around the streets ready to throw over anyone they meet.

(A child takes the bucket containing the torn paper and throws it over the audience – pretending it's water!)

Sometimes people use water pistols instead, or stand by the side of the road with hosepipes ready to give passers by a quick squirt!

(A small group of children squirt each other with water pistols – if they are going to contain water, make sure children taking part have a change of clothing and use really tiny water pistols – like you get in Christmas crackers)

People have a lot of fun and don't mind getting wet as it's so hot.

In Russia, people like to celebrate New Year with a special New Year's tree. Just like Christmas trees, they are decorated with sweets and topped with a bright star.

(A group of children come forward to place small sweets and a star on the tree)

In Russia, children look forward to a special visitor at New Year, he brings presents for all the good children, but it's not Santa, it's Father Frost, and he arrives with his granddaughter, the Snow Girl. Father Frost looks very much like Santa, and although he sometimes wears a red outfit, Father Frost often prefers blue or white which look more frosty.

(1 boy wearing a father Frost hat and 1 girl wearing a snow Girl hat – see 'Make it!' section – hand out the presents to a few children in the group)

Next, there is a special family meal which will usually include meat, green peas, pickles, onions, carrots and potatoes.

(All children hold up paper plates on which they have made their special celebration meal – see 'Make it!' section)

The last country we are looking at today is Australia, which although a very long way away, celebrates New Year very similar to people in England, although there is one special way the people in Australia like to welcome in the New Year – As the clock strikes twelve on New Year's Eve, people come out of their houses blowing whistles, tooting car horns, ringing bells and shaking rattles – anything that makes a lot of noise!

(Teacher beats twelve bongs on the xylophone, then children all make lots of noise with their instruments)

This brings us to the end of our New Year performance. Thank you to everyone for sharing it with us. We hope you all enjoyed it – And a very Happy New Year to you all!

(All children stand and take a bow)

Glittery rainbow rainmaker shakers

These musical instruments are not only beautiful, they're easy to make and children love them.

They can be shaken vigorously to make lots of noise, or trickled gently to give a lovely rainfall effect – experiment with the sounds.

You can either colour the rice yourself the night before and have it ready for children to use, or make this a two-day activity, with children colouring the rice one day and finishing their rainmakers the next.

You will need:

- 1 empty plastic bottle with lid (small pop bottle) per rainmaker

- Dry white rice

- Food colouring in 3 or 4 colours

- Glitter

- Funnel.

Method:

Mix 3 tablespoons of water with enough food colouring to give the desired strength of colour – use an old bowl as food colouring can stain, and mix until colouring is dissolved.

Next, add 1 cup of rice and stir until all rice is well coloured – leave to stand for 5 minutes, stirring occasionally.

Drain the rice and spread on several layers of newspaper to dry, preferably overnight. Repeat with the other food colours.

Next, use a funnel to carefully pour some coloured rice into your plastic bottle, mixing up the colours – experiment a bit with the amount of rice as the sound produced will depend on how much is used. Add some glitter, and put lid back on nice and tight.

Try tipping gently and then more vigorously to make different rainy sounds.

For a bit of extra fun, try cutting out a couple of tiny characters from stiff paper, something like a little bear or cat shape, and put these in the bottle with the rice and glitter, or put in a couple of tiny plastic toys or charms – have fun seeing then appear and disappear in the rice.

To extend this activity you could read children a story, or make one up, which has lots of 'rainy bits' in it, or tell a simple version of the Noah's ark story – plenty of rain in that one!

Links to learning – EYFS Development Matters

The focus of this chapter is looking at the ways people all over the world like to celebrate by having fun with family and friends. Although the activities cover the criteria for many areas of learning as set out in the Development Matters guidelines, they are probably best suited to the areas of Personal, Social and Emotional Development, Understanding the World and Expressive Arts and Design. These areas are covered comprehensively here, looking specifically at the 40-60+ months age group and categories of learning.

Personal, Social and Emotional Development – Self-confidence and self-awareness

A Unique Child

Confident to speak to others about own needs, wants, interests and opinions.
Can describe self in positive terms and talk about abilities.

Early Learning Goal

Children are confident to try new activities, and say why they like some activities more than others. They are confident to speak in a familiar group, will talk about their

ideas, and will choose the resources they need for their chosen activities.

They say when they do or don't need help.

Understanding the World – The World

A Unique Child

Looks closely at similarities, differences, patterns and change.

Early Learning Goal

Children know about similarities and differences in relation to places, objects, materials and living things.

They talk about the features of their own immediate environment and how environments might vary from one another. They make observations of animals and plants and explain why some things occur, and talk about changes.

Expressive Arts and Design – Being Imaginative

A Unique Child

Create simple representations of events, people and objects

Initiates new combinations of movement and gesture in order to express and respond to feelings, ideas and experiences

Chooses particular colours to use for a purpose

Introduces a storyline or narrative into their play

Plays alongside other children who are engaged in the same theme

Plays cooperatively as part of a group to develop and act out a narrative.

Early Learning Goal

Children use what they have learnt about media and materials in original ways, thinking about uses and purposes. They represent their own ideas, thoughts and feelings through design and technology, art, music, dance, role play and stories.

February: Chinese New Year

Over a sixth of the world's population celebrate Chinese New Year. Customs vary in different parts of the world, but the underlying theme is the same – a time to remember family and friends and wish for **peace, prosperity and good fortune** throughout the coming year.

Chinese New Year, also known as the Spring Festival, can fall anytime between late January and mid-February. The Chinese people use the lunar calendar to determine the correct date, which should correspond to the new moon (black moon).

Celebrations will traditionally last for fifteen days, ending with the beautiful **Lantern Festival**. On this day, families walk the streets carrying illuminated lanterns, many being intricate works of art painted with flowers, birds and animal designs. Lanterns are also hung in temples, and carried on a special parade under the light of the full moon. This day is also known as the Chinese Valentine's Day.

During the New Year celebrations, families typically hang lights outside their homes (rather like our Christmas fairy lights) and on New Year's Eve, red and gold decorations are often hung from front doors, incorporating messages of good fortune. These messages will characteristically contain four Chinese characters – called Hui Chun, with typical messages being, prosperity, and long life. House doors themselves are often given a new lick of red paint – for a bit of extra good luck!

Chinese New Year traditions

Lucky colours

Red and gold are the traditional colours of Chinese New Year. Gold is used because it represents wealth, and red, both because it is thought to be a lucky colour and also, because

The story of the twelve Chinese Zodiac Animals

The history of the Chinese zodiac is based on the Chinese lunar calendar, which runs on a twelve year cycle, giving each of the twelve years a name of an animal. The Chinese zodiac is also associated with Chinese astrology and ancient religion, one influential religion being Taoism, which uses planetary constellations to determine a person's future, and also Buddhism – the most widely practised religion in China.

Reincarnation is an important concept of Buddhist belief, with the doctrine being that all animals can be reborn as humans and all humans reborn as animals. This belief has given birth to many stories where animals and humans communicate on equal terms, with animals bestowed with human qualities, as in the story of the Chinese zodiac. In some versions of the zodiac story it is Buddha who calls upon the animals, and not the Taoist God; the Jade Emperor.

There's more than one version of the zodiac story, but the following is one of the most popular, and very similar to many of the other versions.

For an interesting Chinese New Year celebration performance – or just for fun, try narrating the following story while children act out the roles of the twelve zodiac animals – plus the cat and the Jade Emperor.

Simply read the story of The Great Race, letting children run through the river as their chosen animal, either singularly or with other animals, according to the story. Use the rainmakers from the previous chapter to make the sound of running water (a role for children not being an animal) plus the animal hats below to make this a real performance piece, or, better still, combine with a lantern festival parade (see page 20) for an authentic Chinese New Year experience.

the colour red is thought to scare away the monster, Nian, who is thought to come out on New Years Eve.

Firecrackers

Traditionally, firecrackers have been a big part of Chinese New Year celebrations. Stemming from the ancient Chinese tradition of filling bamboo canes with gunpowder to create small explosions in the hope of driving away evil spirits, the practice evolved into the use of shop-bought firecrackers.

Each firecracker is rolled in red paper and they are usually found strung together in long lines to create a sustained and very loud noise. These days the use of firecrackers is mostly restricted to public displays due to many unfortunate accidents.

Red envelopes

It is a Chinese custom for older generations to give red envelopes containing money to children and young people during the New Year celebrations.

The envelopes should be given and received using both hands, as the giving and receiving of gifts is seen as a solemn act requiring a traditional approach – they should also not be opened in front of the giver.

Making the river

If you can find a long piece of blue or blue/green fabric, you can create a great river for children to swim through. I have always found this one of the most popular drama games to use with young children, and all you need is two adults, each holding an end of the fabric. Children can then run through the fabric as it's waved up and down like waves on the sea. Use this idea for all sorts of drama games, for example; King Cnut commanding the tide to halt and not wet his feet, while you gradually bring the wave closer and closer.

Warm-up activity

See **Animal Moves** from warm-up section on page 82.

The Great Race *(teacher to narrate)*

Many, many years ago, the Emperor of Heaven, the Jade Emperor, decided there should be a way of measuring time. So on his birthday he gathered all the animals together and told them that there was to be a swimming race. The first twelve animals across the river would be the winners and would have a year named after them.

All the animals lined up on the riverbank ready for the swimming race. The cat and the rat were side by side as they were good friends, and they were both quite worried about the race because they were not very good swimmers, but, they were clever, and had a good idea – they asked the strong and kindly ox if he would let them sit on his back as he swam across the river. "Of course you can", said the ox, "I'd be glad to help".

As soon as the race started, the ox took the lead, quickly swimming across the river with the cat and the rat sitting on his back. The ox was just about to reach the bank when the rat pushed the cat into the water! The poor cat was left struggling to swim. And, just as the ox was about to win the race, the rat jumped up onto the ox's head and onto the riverbank – winning the race!

"Well done rat" said the Jade Emperor, "The first year shall be named after you."

Because he had been tricked by the rat, Ox took second place, and had the second year named after him.

Next to arrive, was Tiger. He was very tired from all the swimming and just managed to scramble onto the riverbank. He had the third year named after him.

A little while later, Rabbit hopped onto the shore. Rabbit had been very clever and hadn't swum across at all. Rabbit had hopped across the river on some stepping stones and then jumped onto a floating log which carried him to the shore. "Well done, clever rabbit!" said the Jade Emperor. The fourth year will be named 'The Year of the Rabbit'.

The next animal to arrive swooped down from the sky. It was the kindly dragon. "I thought you would win the race", said the Jade Emperor, sounding very surprised. "You can fly and swim very quickly".

"I was about to fly across, when I saw some people and animals looking for clean water to drink", the dragon explained. "So I used magic to make them some rain. Then, I saw a dear little rabbit, floating in the water, so I blew him to the river bank so he would be safe".

"You are very kind", said the Jade Emperor. "The fifth year will be named after you".

The next animal to be seen was the horse. But just as he reached the riverbank, a sneaky snake wriggled in front of him. The snake had been curled around one of the horse's hooves and the poor horse was so surprised to see him, he jumped back into the water, giving the snake a chance to take sixth place in the race. The seventh year was named after the horse.

Next, three animals arrived all together, they were the goat, the monkey and the rooster, and they floated to the riverbank on a raft. They explained to the Emperor that the rooster had found the raft and the monkey and goat had cleared away weeds and pushed the raft to the shore. The Emperor said: "I'm very pleased to see you all working together", adding: "The eighth year will be named after the goat, the ninth year named after the monkey and the rooster will have the tenth year named after him".

The next animal to finish the race was the dog. "You are one of the best swimmers, what took you so long?" Asked the Jade Emperor.

"I stopped to have a bath on the way", explained the dog. "The river was so fresh and clean".

"Well done anyway!" Said the Emperor; you shall have the eleventh year named after you.

Now there was just one place left. Which animal would have the last year named after him? Finally, a grunting noise could be heard, and the pig clambered up the riverbank.

"Pig, you took a very long time to cross the river, what took you so long?" Asked the Emperor. "Oh, I was very hungry and stopped to have a snack", explained the pig. "And after my snack, I felt very sleepy, so I had a little nap"

"Well congratulations Pig, you shall have the twelfth and last year named after you."

And that is how the twelve years of the Chinese zodiac got their names. As for the cat who had been pushed into the water by the rat, well, he finally managed to crawl out of the water, but was far too late to have a year named after him. He was so cross with the rat, he never forgave him, and ever since that day, cats and rats have never been friends.

The Chinese zodiac has followed the same cycle of years ever since, with each of the twelve years being named after one of the twelve animals winning the race.

Chinese Zodiac animal hats

These really simple to make headband style hats, are all the costume that's needed to put on a special Chinese New Year celebration of your own. Have an example set of paper plate animal faces ready-made, so children get an idea of how to draw theirs, it makes choosing their animal more fun too.

You will need:

- 1 strip of card for head band – approximately 60cm x 9cm

- 1 paper plate

- Chunky felt tips or markers.

Method:

Once children have decided which animal they'd like to be, let them design their headband accordingly – just colouring in with a suitable colour is fine.

Next, let children draw their chosen animal's face onto their paper plate. You can have some additional bits ready cut out for gluing onto the faces if you like, and it does give a nice effect – bits like a snake's tongue, a pig's nose, two big teeth for the rat, ears for the rabbit, monkey, horse, dog and tiger, horns for the ox, beak and feathers for the rooster, cotton wool for the sheep, horns and big nostrils for the dragon.

Staple animal face to the centre of headband, taking care that no sharp bits of staple poke out, then fit band to child's head and staple to secure.

Get everyone ready for the animal parade!

Chinese New Year paper plate tambourines

Perfect for a marching band, these musical instruments are simple enough for young children to make and are great for shaking in a parade. Children can decorate their plates as they wish, no need to be neat with this one.

You will need:

- 2 paper plates each

- Crayons/felt-tips/stickers/glitter, for decoration

- Long paper streamers/tinsel/ribbons

- Dried beans or similar – but don't use anything too small, as it will fall through gaps too easily

- Stapler.

Method:

Decorate underside of both paper plates as desired.

Place paper plates together to make a 'flying saucer' shape with a gap in the middle. Staple edges together, leaving a gap for filling.

Fill with anything suitably rattily and staple shut. Staple on streamers – have a good rattle!

Lantern Festival parade

A lantern parade around a playground or outside area is a lovely way of marking Chinese New Year.

You could combine a parade together with a performance of The Great Race, but it makes a nice, simple performance piece on its own, and just enough for younger children. Maybe pick one or more of the craft activities detailed here, to make the parade extra special

Making the lanterns

You will need:

- Coloured paper or gift wrapping paper – A4 size

- Little sticks for holding lanterns – flower support stakes, or similar
- Strips of plain paper with riddles pre-written – riddle on one side, answer on the back
- Orange, red and yellow tissue
- Scissors
- Sticky tape or stapler
- Glue sticks.

Some fun riddles

During the lantern festival, it is customary for people to guess the answer to lantern riddles which are usually given in the form of a poem, word or phrase and which are written on the lanterns.

It is said that guessing these riddles is as hard as 'fighting with a tiger' giving lantern riddles another name – 'Lantern Tigers'.

Some easy children's riddles

Which is faster hot or cold?
Hot is faster – you can catch a cold!

What kind of cookies do baby monkeys have with their milk?
Chocolate chimp!

Why was the ghost driving the fire engine?
He was a fire-frighter!

What goes up a chimney down, but won't come down a chimney up?
An Umbrella!

What is the world's most valuable fish?
A Goldfish!

What is full of holes but still holds water?
A sponge!

What do you call a witch who lives at the beach?
A sand-witch!

How do you make a tissue dance?
You put a little boogie in it!

What goes up brown or white and comes down yellow and white
An egg!

Why couldn't the bicycle stand up by itself?
It was two-tyred!

Method:

Fold paper in half and cut about 12 slits along the fold, being careful not to cut too close to the edge. Unfold and tape or staple the short edges of the paper together.

Cut a strip of paper approximately 6 inches long and staple to one end of the lantern as a handle.

Roughly cut or tear some tissue paper into flame shaped pieces and staple or tape inside the lantern.

Staple one of the paper riddle strips to the bottom of the lantern, so it hangs underneath.

Attach lantern to a short stick for carrying.

Which animal are you?

Just for fun, you can work out children's animal zodiac sign from the chart above:

Chinese animal year chart

Rat	1960	1972	1984	1996	2008
Ox	1961	1973	1985	1997	2009
Tiger	1962	1974	1986	1998	2010
Rabbit	1963	1975	1987	1999	2011
Dragon	1964	1976	1988	2000	2012
Snake	1965	1977	1989	2001	2013
Horse	1966	1978	1990	2002	2014
Sheep	1967	1979	1991	2003	2015
Monkey	1968	1980	1992	2004	2016
Rooster	1969	1981	1993	2005	2017
Dog	1970	1982	1994	2006	2018
Pig	1971	1983	1995	2007	2019

The Story of Nian, the terrible monster

This popular, ancient Chinese New Year story, is a traditional children's favourite and is also a great story to use during a drama session. Start by reading the story to children, then let them prowl, crawl and creep about as their own horrible monster, telling them that when you blow a whistle, shake a tambourine or wave a red scarf, they must all run away scared to the back of the hall – their cave.

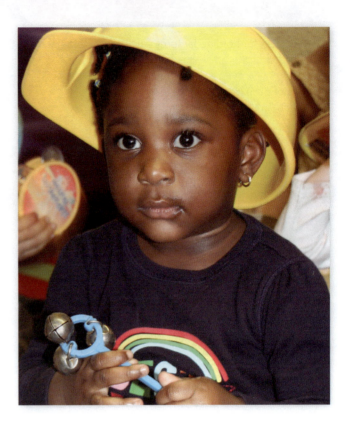

Once upon a time, long, long ago, there lived a horrible, terrible, scary monster, and his name was Nian.

Once every year, this monster would visit a little village and SCARE everyone!

This was terrible, and all the villagers wanted to stop Nian, but he was so scary, they just didn't know what they could do, until one day, when just by luck, they discovered that Nian was frightened of a couple of things himself. He was scared of the colour red and most of all; he was scared of loud noises.

All the villagers had a meeting and decided to make red banners and noise makers, so that when Nian came to scare them, they could frighten him away.

The villagers waited and waited, and then one day, Nian was seen making his way towards their village. Quick as could be, all the villagers grabbed their red banners and noise makers and ran around the village with them, waving the banners and shaking and banging the noisy instruments.

Nian was so scared; he ran away and was never seen or heard from ever again!

Which all goes to explain the Chinese New Year tradition of shaking noise makers and letting off firecrackers, and why the colour red is thought to be such a lucky colour, bringing joy and luck.

At the stroke of midnight, things get very noisy in China – just in case Nian should put in an appearance once again!

You can extend the 'monsters' topic in all sorts of ways, and it is a really good one to use with this age group as children can give full reign to their imaginations – who's to say what a monster looks like?

Try cutting out lots of big simple shapes from coloured scrap paper which can be used for heads and bodies, pre-cut some long strips of paper and fold concertina style to use as wiggly arms and legs, and bring out the bits and pieces box

for decoration. Just let children create a monster to their own design. I find this kind of unstructured, child initiated craft topic is often the most enjoyable and rewarding for pre-school children. It is a chance to explore lots of colours, shapes and textures of materials – also a chance to get their hands on those sparkly sequins they've had their eyes on, but as yet have had no opportunity to use

Links to learning – EYFS Development Matters

This chapter focuses on working together, and thoroughly covers the areas of Personal, Social and Emotional Development, Expressive Arts and Design and Understanding the World through all categories of learning.

(Looking specifically at the 40-60+ months age group.)

Personal, Social and Emotional Development – Making Relationships

A Unique Child

Initiates conversations, attends to and takes account of what others say.

Explains own knowledge and understanding, and asks appropriate questions of others.

Takes steps to resolve conflicts with other children, e.g. finding a compromise.

Early Learning Goal

Children play co-operatively, taking turns with others. They take account of one another's ideas about how to organise their activity. They show sensitivity to others' needs and feelings, and form positive relationships with adults and other children.

Expressive Arts and Design – Exploring and Using Media and Materials

A Unique Child

Begins to build a repertoire of songs and dances.

Explores the different sounds of instruments.

Explores what happens when they mix colours.

Experiments to create different textures.

Understands that different media can be combined to create new effects. Manipulates materials to achieve a planned effect.

Constructs with a purpose in mind, using a variety of resources.

Uses simple tools and techniques competently and appropriately.

Selects appropriate resources and adapts work where necessary.

Selects tools and techniques needed to shape, assemble and join materials they are using.

Early Learning Goal

Children sing songs, make music and dance, and experiment with ways of changing them. They safely use and explore a variety of materials, tools and techniques, experimenting with colour, design, texture, form and function.

Understanding the World – The World

A Unique Child

Looks closely at similarities, differences, patterns and change.

Early Learning Goal

Children know about similarities and differences in relation to places, objects, materials and living things. They talk about the features of their own immediate environment and how environments might vary from one another. They make observations of animals and plants and explain why some things occur, and talk about changes.

March: Holi – festival of colours

The Hindu festival of Holi is a truly beautiful time of celebration. Chiefly observed in India and countries with large Hindu populations, Holi is primarily a **celebration of springtime**, the season's beautiful colours, and a farewell to winter months, but originally marked the agricultural season of the Rabi (agricultural) crops. Although Holi has religious roots with connections to Hindu mythology, for most Hindus today, Holi is the least religious of Hindu celebrations – a time for lots of fun, and also a time when the usual boundaries between young and old and rich and poor are lowered (although not completely ignored) in favour of a time of mutual celebration.

In most regions Holi celebrations last about two days, being celebrated on the last full moon day of the lunar month;

Phalg una (February/March), with Rangapanchami (fifth day of the full moon) marking the official end of Holi.

There are certain well-established customs attached to Holi. The main custom is the smearing of coloured powders on the faces of friends and family and the throwing of coloured and scented water – hence the name **Festival of Colours**. Another popular custom on the first day of Holi is to participate in the building of a large public bonfire. It is customary for men to prepare for this by hunting for and collecting wood. The bonfire is lit as the moon rises, close to midnight.

Traditionally, natural colours made from plants were used to make the coloured dyes used during the Holi celebrations, but today synthetic colours are widely used, together with coloured foams and balloons filled with coloured water – great for popping on your victim's head!

A very messy festival!

Holi is a time of fun for young and old and traditionally very messy, with people throwing powdered paint at each other – friends, neighbours and strangers in the street are all fair game and the air is often bright with clouds of coloured powder.

Gulal and Abeer

Gulal is a powdered colour found in plentiful supply in Indian markets in the days leading up to Holi.

Abeer is made of small crystals of mica and is used to make coloured powders sparkly.

Pichkaris

The use of water pistols and long syringes (pichkaris) are a modern take on the throwing of coloured water and very useful for squirting over distance. Water-filled balloons and water bombs are also very popular during the Holi festival.

Tesu

Originally, the coloured powders and liquids were made from drying and grinding natural ingredients. The flowers from the tesu tree gave a very popular and effective orange-red colour, once dried and ground to a fine powder and mixed with water.

Holi performance piece

This story is actually a Brazilian fable, but its colour theme makes it perfect to use when looking at Holi, and it's a lovely story to use as the basis for a simple performance piece with your children either in a hall or playground. Try reading through to familiarise children with the story, then have a few practice tries with you narrating and children acting it out.

The costume activity ideas are easy and fun to make, and the story lends itself well to both small and large groups of children – as many beetles as you like!

Warm-up activity

See **Animal Moves** and **Emotions** from the warm-up section on page 82.

Things to do

- Gather together the essential resources listed – making any changes to suit your own requirements along the way.

- Be sure to check out the 'Make it!' section for instructions on making some of the (very simple) costume and prop pieces.

- Use the simple script to narrate the story – following the performance instructions for children's parts.

Get everyone involved – Have fun!

Essential resources

(See **Make it!** section below)

- Animal headbands

- Tail for Rat

- Beetle coats.

Make it!

Jungle animal headbands

Keep things nice and simple. Just use strips of card approximately 12cm wide, which can be taped to fit round a child's head.

Next, let children choose which jungle animal they would like to be for the performance, but which will need to include a few beetles, a rat and a parrot.

All that's needed for the beetles are two pipe-cleaner antennae taped to the band which should be coloured in grey.

For the parrot, make a few coloured paper feathers to tape to the band, which should also be multi-coloured.

For the rat, make brown furry ears and colour the band brown.

All other children can pick which jungle animal they would like to be and make a headband to match – some ideas could be:

- A tiger – stripy ears and headband

How the beetle got her colours

Many, many years ago, all beetles were just plain grey – they couldn't be found in all the beautiful colours we find them in today.

A child dressed in grey or dull colours, and wearing a beetle headband crawls onto the stage.

One of these little grey beetles lived near a big rat, who was a great, big, bully and teased the little beetle every day.

A child dressed as rat scampers onto the stage, swinging his brown tail.

"You're so ugly", Rat would say, and "Grey is such a boring colour. I have a lovely brown fur coat, the Jaguar has a beautiful golden coat with black spots, and Mrs Parrot's feathers are blue and red and yellow and green, but you – are just plain grey. I wish you would hide in the bushes, so I didn't have to see you". Then Rat would scurry away chuckling to himself.

Rat chuckles to himself as he scurries away, and the little grey beetle looks very sad.

Now every day, when Mrs Parrot was sitting high up in the trees, she would hear Rat teasing the little grey beetle and it made her feel angry – very angry! She liked the little beetle very much, and she made a plan to teach Rat a lesson.

The next day, when Rat was being unkind to the little beetle, Mrs Parrot flew down.

A child wearing a parrot headband and bright clothing flies onto the stage.

Mrs Parrot said: "I have an idea Rat. Why don't you and beetle have a race and I will give the winner a prize – a beautiful new coat. Then if beetle wins, she won't be plain anymore".

Rat laughed and laughed. *Rat laughs loudly, holding his sides.*

"Beetle won't win!" He said: "I can run much faster than her. I have four strong legs, she only has six silly little legs to scurry about on. I'll win for sure, but I will race you beetle – it will be fun to see you lose!".

Well, word of the race spread throughout the jungle, and all the jungle animals turned up to see Rat and Beetle have their race.

All children wearing their animal headbands gather round to watch the race, with two animals holding the finish tape at the winning line.

Well, the race began. Rat raced into the lead, imagining the lovely new coat he was about to win, and wondering what colour it would be; red or blue, violet or gold – or maybe rainbow colored stripes…

Rat had a quick look behind him, but as he thought, the little beetle was nowhere to be seen. "Oh, how I'll laugh at that silly beetle when I finish the race" he said to himself. "She will be way behind me. It will take her ages to reach the finish line on those tiny little legs."

But – can you guess what happened next?

Beetle flies, arms outstretched like wings, to the finish line and wins the race. All the animals cheer.

When Rat reached the finish line, there was Beetle, waiting for him. She had won the race!

Rat scampers to the winning line.

Rat was very shocked and very, very angry. "I don't believe it" he moaned. "How did you get to the finish line before me – you've only got tiny, little legs!"

Mrs Parrot, Rat and Beetle stand in front of the other animals – Rat looks angry But Mrs Parrot and Beetle are smiling.

"I flew Mr Rat – I flew." The little grey beetle said smiling. "You flew – I didn't know you could fly!" Shouted the angry rat.

Mrs Parrot laughed and laughed and said: "Rat, you should never judge other people by the way they look. They may not look special, but they may have skills you do not". Rat stomped off into the forest, grumbling all the way.

Rat stomps off stage.

And the little beetle? Well, she chose a beautiful new coat, as green as leaves and as golden as sunshine.

Mrs Parrot gives Beetle her beautiful new coat and Beetle puts it on.

And, if you're very lucky, you just might see a beetle with beautiful green and gold colours on its back – just like these!

All beetles come to the front, twirling round to show off their beautiful beetle coats.

- A butterfly – colour and cut out a butterfly shape and a multi-coloured headband

- A zebra – black and white stripy pointed ears and a striped headband.

An alternative would be to use printed images of jungle animal's heads taken from the Internet which can be cut out and fixed to the headbands. This does give a wider choice as you can use animals that might be a bit tricky for children to create themselves.

Beetle coats

The easiest way to make the beetle's coats (representing the lovely green and gold colours seen on some types of beetle) is to cut one green and one gold shiny paper rounded-oblong shape per child and attach these to an old cardigan or jumper – to represent the wing case of the beetle.

Other props

Rat's tail – Something long and swishy. You could use a long piece of brown fur fabric if available, but if not, an old brown cardigan belt or something similar will do.

Finishing tape – A long scarf will do nicely.

More ideas for Holi

Take a look at the following ideas for colour-themed activities which are both simple to set up and low on resources.

Set up a colour-themed interest table

Try setting up a colour themed interest table for Holi week. Ask children to bring in small objects of a specific colour from home, changing the colour daily. End the week with a rainbow theme, asking for multi-coloured objects showing as many different colours as possible, with children themselves – and nursery staff – being dressed in multi-coloured clothes. Interest tables such as this are always popular as children love to share objects from home. Make a point of talking about the objects brought in, spending a bit of time looking at the table each day.

Make a big rainbow hand-print picture

You will need:

- Water-based paint in primary colours, plus extra colours if available

- Chunky paintbrushes

- Long roll of plain paper.

Method:

This is a great activity to take outside on a sunny day. It works best with a roll of wall-lining paper, as children can keep on printing with lots of room to make their prints. Help children paint their hands if they ask for help, but if not, just give them free rein of the paints and paper, pointing out new colours that emerge as paints and prints overlap.

Handprint Butterflies

You will need:

- White A4 paper

- Water based paint in various colours

- Felt-tipped pen.

Method:

Fold your sheet of A4 paper in half and open up. Paint children's hands in any colours they like and make an open hand print, palm close to the fold. Fold paper over and press to give a second mirror print of the hand. Open up –

creating a bit of excitement around the big reveal, and see the beautiful butterfly emerge! Once dry, you can use a felt-tipped pen to add little feelers, a smiley face, anything you fancy.

Try making two hand prints, one under the other, for a double wing effect.

Marble paint roll

You will need:

- Tray – deeper ones are better

- 3 or 4 marbles placed in individual bowls of paint

- Water based paint in various colours in separate bowls

- A4 white paper.

Method:

Place a sheet of paper in your tray. Roll a marble around in its bowl and using a spoon, place in the tray. Now the fun bit – help children roll the marble around by tilting the tray to create lovely lines of colour.

Add extra marbles and different colours of paint to create a lovely rainbow effect as the lines overlap.

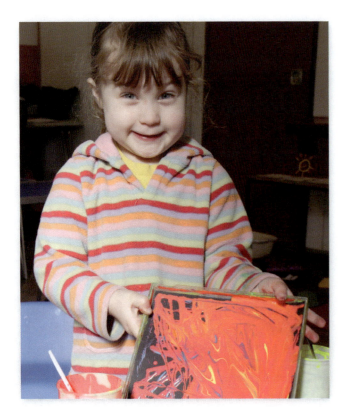

Links to learning – EYFS Development Matters

The use of colour is the predominant theme in this chapter, which comprehensively covers the area of Expressive Arts and Design as follows (looking specifically at the 40-60+months age group).

Expressive Arts and Design – Exploring and Using media and Materials

A Unique Child

Explores what happens when they mix colours.

Experiments to create different textures.

Understands that different media can be combined to create new effects.

Manipulates materials to achieve a planned effect. Constructs with a purpose in mind, using a variety of resources.

Uses simple tools and techniques competently and appropriately.

Selects appropriate resources and adapts work where necessary.

Selects tools and techniques needed to shape, assemble and join materials they are using.

Early Learning Goal

Children sing songs, make music and dance, and experiment with ways of changing them. They safely use and explore a variety of materials, tools and techniques, experimenting with colour, design, texture, form and function.

April: Easter

Easter is a Christian festival celebrating the **resurrection of Jesus Christ**, and is the most important of all Christian festivals. The date of Easter is not fixed, it changes each year, though as a general rule, Easter Sunday falls on the first Sunday following the first full moon after 21st March.

Easter is not an isolated holiday, but the culmination of the season of **Lent**, and is actually a focal point for a number of separate but connected religious commemorations.

Shrove Tuesday

Otherwise known as **Pancake Day**, Shrove Tuesday falls immediately before the start of Lent. Traditionally, pancakes are eaten on this day as a way of using up foods such as fats and eggs, which are forbidden during Lent – so also a last chance to indulge yourself. As a way of marking Shrove Tuesday, you could swap your usual fruit snack for mini pancakes – they're not expensive or messy and there's no need to heat them up; just hand out straight from the packet.

Lent

In the Christian calendar, Lent is the period of forty days before Easter. It is traditionally a time of reflection and fasting.

Ash Wednesday

Being the first day of Lent, Ash Wednesday falls somewhere between February 4th and March 11th and acts as a reminder of the forty days Jesus spent fasting in the desert in mental preparation of his death. Because of this, in the Catholic and Anglican churches Ash Wednesday is often followed by a period of fasting, though today it is sometimes restricted to Ash Wednesday and Good Friday.

The Holy Week of Easter

Holy week starts with Palm Sunday and ends with Easter Sunday, celebrating the resurrection of Jesus. It incorporates Maundy Thursday, marking the last supper of Jesus Christ and Good Friday, marking his crucifixion. It is traditionally a time for Christians to devote some time contemplating the suffering, death and eventual resurrection of Jesus Christ.

Palm Sunday

Also sometimes referred to as Passion Sunday, Palm Sunday marks the first day of Holy Week which ends with Easter Sunday. It marks Jesus' entry into Jerusalem prior to his crucifixion.

Whit Sunday or Pentecost

Falling on the first Sunday after Easter, Whit Sunday is rarely observed today, but would have been celebrated for up to a week in the Middle Ages, when various pagan traditions were incorporated such as May Pole dancing. The celebration marks the coming of the Holy Spirit in the form of flames to his followers, fifty days after his resurrection. The word 'Pentecost', comes from the Greek for fiftieth.

Celebrating Easter

For many families, Easter is a very significant religious occasion, and for many others, more a time for family and fun. But whether celebrated at home in a religious manner or not, the fun aspects and religious side of Easter sit easily together and the following activities should be suitable for all children in your group.

Have an Easter Egg hunt!

An Easter Egg hunt is the highlight of many Easter celebrations. This year, why not hold an Easter Egg hunt fun-day, that's not only got a few surprises up its sleeve, but also some fun challenges that involve team work, problem solving and motor skills? Turn the celebrations into a week-long fun-packed Easter extravaganza!

Planning for the hunt

The first thing you'll need to think about when planning your hunt, is how you will ensure all children get a fair share of treats. Probably the easiest way to go about this is to have children hunt in small groups, with adults in charge having a few extra treats handy to secretly hide for any children not lucky enough to find many. Also, tell children that you will

make sure everyone goes home with some treats at the end of the day – to save any tears. I say treats rather than eggs, because although you will want to include them, you can also hide some little gifts such as decorative tiny fluffy chicks. Local one-pound shops and markets are sure to have some suitable little bits and bobs. Although the eggs and gifts should be fairly inexpensive, you can ask for a small money donation from parents – but do keep it minimal.

Ideas and tips

- It's nice if children have an Easter basket to collect their treasure in and an Easter bonnet to wear, both of which can be easily made with children in advance (see **Make it!** section, page 31).

- In case you have to postpone the hunt in the event of rain, keep a couple of days free in advance.

- Prepare the hunting area in advance by putting out some objects that will be good for hiding things in and under – watering can, dolls pram, flower pots…

- Make it a special occasion by handing out proper, individually named invitations, instead of the usual letter home.

- Ask parents if children can come into nursery dressed in yellow, green or pink – spring colours.

- Invite parents to come into nursery a bit before home time for a simple Easter bonnet and baskets parade around the playground or outside space. Just let children walk or march whilst singing 'The Grand old Duke of York', in a big circle, showing off their handmade crafts.

- Help children to find treasure by giving the time honoured – you're getting warmer or colder clues – but do explain how this works first.

Egg and spoon obstacle course

As part of your Easter celebrations, an Easter Egg and spoon race makes a fun physical activity that uses both fine and gross motor skills, plus lots of hand-eye coordination. Use small, foil-wrapped chocolate eggs instead of real eggs – less fuss, more fun, and use big spoons to make it easier.

The first thing to do is have a think about the obstacles you will be using for your course, which will obviously depend on available space. Some ideas for obstacles could be:

- Cones placed on the floor to weave in and out of, or two beams placed side by side, leaving just a small gap – so children have to turn sideways to walk through

- Bending down to pick up a beanbag and throwing it in a bucket

- Stepping in and out of hoops placed on the floor

- Ducking under a pole held by two adults

- Child walks whilst balancing a beanbag on their head (holding it on with one hand).

Some of these ideas might sound a bit tricky for this age group, considering they will be balancing an egg on a spoon at the same time, but that's all good – it's more fun, so when their egg falls off they can just pick it up and put it back on again and carry on with the course. At the end they can put their chocolate egg in their basket ready for home time. Have some spares to replace any eggs that get dropped so often, their foil comes off.

Bunny-hop race

Both loads of fun and great physical exercise, a bunny-hop race is good for practising balancing skills. Make it extra fun by letting children wear bunny ears (see **Make it!** section, page 32).

Before you can have a bunny-hop race, you need to be able to bunny-hop. So get children practising this before

race day. Keep the whole thing really low key and fun, as some children find this kind of physical activity much harder than others.

Mark out starting and finishing lines with chalk.

Divide children into small groups of about four or five.

Start the race with a ready, steady, go, and first bunny over the finishing line wins – but give everyone a little prize to take home – you can't beat bubbles!

Make it!

Easter bonnets

These are the easiest type of bonnet to make (not really a bonnet, but fun to make).

The easiest way to go about these is to start with a simple strip of thin card for each child – approximately 12cm wide and long enough to fit around head with a bit of overlap.

Children can either decorate these with scrap-box bits and pieces; glitter, feathers, shiny paper – whatever you've got, or you can supply some special Easter pictures to colour, cut out and stick to bonnets.

Chocolate Easter nests

A great Easter alternative to the chocolate rice-crispy cake – quick, easy and delicious.

Makes 30

You will need:

- Shredded wheat (normal sized box of 16)

- 400g milk chocolate (cheap supermarket own brand is great for this)

- Cake cases

- 2 bags mini eggs for decoration

- Some little decorative chicks (optional).

Method:

Crumble cereal into a big bowl

Melt the chocolate in a microwave, pour in bowl and give a good stir

Using a teaspoon, dollop mixture into cake cases, using the spoon to press a little dimple in the middle, so it looks like a little nest.

Put two or three eggs in each nest

Put in the fridge to cool

Add a little chick to each nest.

Easter bonnet biscuits

You will need:

- Rich tea biscuits (1 per bonnet)

- 1 box of icing sugar

- Marshmallows (1 per bonnet)

- Little sweets or cake decorations.

Method:

Mix some icing sugar with water to give a gluey paste

Use a blob of icing sugar to stick a marshmallow to the centre of each biscuit

Use more icing to stick little sweets or cake decorations to bonnet.

Note: Be sure to check for food allergies before cooking activities and have plenty of soft drinks or drinking water available for the more physical activities, especially if it's a hot day.

Staple a simple card handle to the basket and put a little bit of shredded green tissue in the bottom – if available. You can also have children leave baskets out overnight for the Easter Bunny to fill with little eggs on the last day of term.

Bunny-ears headband

Start with a simple strip of thin, white card (see Easter bonnets above).

Cut out two bunny ears from brown or white card. You might like to cut out smaller ear shapes from pink paper for the inside of the ears to make them a bit fancy.

Help children draw two pink eyes, a bunny nose and whiskers on their card strip and stick on two big bunny teeth.

Staple headbands together to give a snug fit and staple ears to back of band – opposite side to bunny face.

Easter Egg cards

These traditional Easter celebration cards are perfect for practising fine motor skills. Making small patterns like

To finish, staple or tape ends together to give a snug fit (an additional strip of card, the same width, can be fixed over the top of the band to form a crown if desired).

Paper plate Easter baskets

These very easy to make baskets are just the right size for little ones to take hunting.

Simply take a paper plate and make a cut from the edge to the centre. Roll up to make a cone and staple together.

Next, decorate with paper flower shapes or something similar, such as lambs, Easter eggs or hot-cross buns.

rows of circles, lines and zigzags forms the beginning of writing skills and poses a real challenge for many pre-school children.

Have Easter cards pre-prepared with a picture of an Easter Egg as big as the card. The more able children can draw patterns on their egg free-hand, but the majority of children will probably benefit from having patterns faintly pre-drawn for tracing over or shown as a series of dots to join up. The idea is to make patterns small, requiring small movement pencil skills. You could make two versions of the card, one with larger patterns to trace over, to cover the differentiation of writing skills in your group.

Once patterns have been drawn, children can colour cards to make them beautiful and trace over the words, 'For my family' inside – and don't forget kisses.

An alternative here could be to have children each decorate an egg as above, but instead of making greetings cards, cut eggs out and use to create a big wall poster.

Cut out or draw a large basket for the bottom of the picture and glue all the decorated eggs on top in a big pile – have children each make an extra egg for taking home, to stop any tears at home time due to leaving their work behind.

How about bringing in a few traditional Easter treats for children to try? Simnel cake and hot cross buns can be cut into pieces so children can have a little taste.

Links to learning – EYFS Development Matters

All the above activities provide opportunities for working on a child's physical development; even the cooking activities, as they require specific fine motor skills – In their crumbling, mixing and sticking, and although many areas of the early years curriculum are covered in this chapter, I have focused here on physical development as it covers all areas so well.

(Looking specifically at the 40-60+ months age group.)

Physical Development – Moving and Handling

A Unique Child

Experiments with different ways of moving.

Jumps off an object and lands appropriately.

Negotiates space successfully when playing racing and chasing games with other children, adjusting speed or changing direction to avoid obstacles.

Travels with confidence and skill around, under, over and through balancing and climbing equipment.

Shows increasing control over an object in pushing, patting, throwing, catching or kicking it.

Uses simple tools to effect changes to materials.
Handles tools, objects, construction and malleable materials safely and with increasing control.

Early Learning Goal

Children show good control and co-ordination in large and small movements.

They move confidently in a range of ways, safely negotiating space. They handle equipment and tools effectively, including pencils for writing.

May: Kodomo no Hi – Children's Day in Japan

Children take centre stage, no school – and fish fly!

Kodomo no Hi (Children's Day) is a Japanese national holiday which takes place on 5th May – the fifth day of the fifth month each year and is part of Japan's 'Golden Week' which includes the celebration of the Emperor's Birthday, Greenery Day, Showa Day, Constitution Memorial Day and Children's Day.

In 1948 the Japanese government decreed Children's Day a national holiday dedicated to the celebration of all children, their personalities and happiness. Until 1948, there were separate holidays for boys and girls, with Tango no Sekku – also known as Boy's Day, or Feast of Banners, for boys, and Hinamatsun – also known as the Japanese Doll Festival, for

girls. It was decided there should be a holiday celebrating all children, both boys and girls, so Tango no Sekku was renamed Kodomo no hi – Children's Day. Today the annual Kodomo no hi festival is eagerly anticipated by children all over Japan.

On this day a traditional koinobori flag in the shape of a carp, (type of fish), is flown for each child in the family. As the breeze gently blows the fish, they look like they are swimming.

Traditional Kodomo no Hi fable

The following simple version of a traditional Japanese fable is great fun to use with young children as part of a drama session or class assembly. The underlying message of perseverance to achieve your goals is a good one to introduce to this age group, and can be used as a platform for circle time conversations about times when children in your group have tried really hard to achieve their goals.

While there are many variations, the following is the basic story of the koinobori (carp streamer).

The story of the Leaping Dragon-Fish

There are two types of dragon; those that are born as dragons, and those that become dragons. The type that turn into dragons start life as a type of fish called carp. They turn into dragons by swimming along China's Yellow River until they reach a special waterfall called the 'Dragon's Gate'.

Some of the carp spring up into the air, trying to reach the higher water above the swirling waterfall, but jumping is very difficult for a fish, and only the carp that try really hard manage to jump up high enough. Those few fish who do manage to reach the water above the waterfall are rewarded for trying so hard by being magically turned into dragons.

The meaning of this story is that if you try very hard and do your best, you will always be able to do the things you try to do – even if they seem very difficult!

Swimming up the river

The following activity would make a lovely, simple assembly piece or use as part of any Kodomo no hi celebration. Have some children play traditional Japanese musical instruments to accompany the activity (see **Make it!** section opposite).

As in February's Making the River activity, a long piece of silky blue or green fabric would make a great river for your children to swim through – with the help of a couple of adults to hold the ends and swish.

Start off with children practising fish movements (see **Animal moves** warm-up activity on page 82), then move on to dragon moves – as fierce as they like, without touching anyone else! Also practise leaping as high as they can, with arms up high and pointy feet.

Next, have children swim through the swirling river, starting off as fish on one side of the room and turning into dragons on the other – not forgetting to jump as high as they can in the middle of the river.

Make it!

Create your own Koinobori streamer

These are really effective when hung in a playground, or open space.

An adult will need to do all the assembling, so make this a group project, making just two or three – children helping with the decorating bits.

Then it's everyone outside to watch them swim through the air!

You can always make a couple of your own in advance.

You will need (per fish):

- 1 A3 sheet heavy paper

- Paints, chunky markers, scrap box scraps or old magazines for decoration

- Glue

- Length of string or ribbon for fixing or holding

- Scraps of tissue paper, crêpe paper or some colourful carrier bags for making streamers

- Stapler

- Hole punch.

Method:

Draw a big fish shape, with an opening for the mouth and tail – at least 15cm wide at each end, with the body being as fat as possible at its widest part.

Cut out so you have two identical fish.

Decorate one side of each fish shape with paint, chunky markers, tissue paper and/or any scraps available. Big fish scale shapes cut from colourful magazine pages work really well. Leave to dry.

Lay first fish decorated side down on table and glue around the edges, but leave the mouth and tail un-glued. Press second fish firmly on top, pressing seams to give a firm seal.

Glue some tissue or crêpe paper streamers to the tail and leave to dry, or cut some streamers from colourful carrier bags.

Fix fish mouth open with a staple at each corner.

Punch a hole on each side of the fish mouth and thread your length of string or ribbon through the holes, tying the ends of the string to the holes.

Now you are ready to hang your traditional Koinobori outside so everyone can watch it swimming through the air. Or, if it's not very windy out, let children take turns to run around with it outdoors, holding it at arm's length, so it floats through the air.

Rice cakes and oak leaves

It is customary in Japan during Children's Day, for families to eat Kashiwa – traditional rice cakes filled with sweet bean paste and wrapped in oak leaves. Although attempting to make the traditional version of kashiwa might prove a bit ambitious with pre-school children, you might like to have a go at this very simple activity, in keeping with the kashiwa tradition.

You will need (per child):

- 1 pre-drawn oak leaf shape

- Colouring pens/pencils/crayons

- 3- 4 mini rice cakes – plain or caramel flavour

- Some oak leaves for children to look at and copy.

Method:

Let children colour their oak leaves before cutting out – less fiddly. Cut out and lightly score down the centre of each leaf, giving each a little fold.

At snack time, let children use their oak leaves as plates, giving each child a few mini rice cakes to place on top – very simple Japanese Kashiwa.

Handprint celebration cards

These fun, handprint celebration cards are a lovely way to mark Children's day, as each handprint is as unique as the child it belongs to.

You will need:

- 1 card per child

- Paints in shallow containers in a selection of colours.

- Little sponges for dabbing paint on hands.

- Simple pre-printed little messages to go inside cards – 'Happy Children's Day to all my family', for example.

Method:

Help children make a nice open-finger handprint on the front of their card, allowing children to choose the colour they like best to make it more personal. Try printing one hand on the front of the card and one inside.

If you stick to the primary colours – red, blue and yellow, plus white, you can use this activity for a bit of colour mixing practice, dabbing on different colours to make greens, pinks and purples.

Add a Happy Children's Day message to the front of the card, then help children add their name next to their hand print by either writing over their name, or writing it for them depending on ability. Let children glue a greeting inside their card to finish off.

While you have children's hands good and painty, why not make an extra set of prints. Cut these out and use to make a display poster representing all the children in your group, using the heading: Kodomo no hi – Happy Children's day!

Make a Japanese flag

The national flag of Japan is represented by a large red disk, representing the sun, on a white rectangle background and is officially called Nisshoki (sun mark flag) in Japan, but is more commonly known as Hinomaru (circle of the sun). Make these very simple, little kiwi-printed Japanese flags to wave on Children's Day. Can children guess what the red circle is supposed to represent?

You will need (per flag):

- 1 sheet of white paper approximately 15cm x 10 ½ cm

- 1 drinking straw

- Red paint

- Sticking tape

- ½ a kiwi fruit for printing – kiwi fruit give a lovely pattern to the circle, but half a potato is also good.

Method:

Pour some red paint onto sponges lying in shallow trays.

Pat the kiwi or potato halves with tissue to dry them off a bit, then help children centre a red circle print on their paper

Roll one end of the paper round a drinking straw and fix in place with sticky tape – Have a good wave!

Traditional Japanese musical instruments to make

Combine the following hand-made musical instruments with any bell type instruments you already have – tambourines, bell sticks and sleigh bells for example, also rainmakers and drums, for children to use in accompaniment to the swimming up the river activity above.

Ichigenkin
The Ichigenkin, 'one-string zither', has a slender, flat body carved from wood and a single silk string which is plucked with a pointed tubular plectrum which is worn on the index finger of the right hand, and a 'rokan' (tubular ivory device) which is worn on the middle finger of the left hand and used to depress the string to vary the pitch.

Children can easily make their own Ichigenkin by simply stretching a rubber band over an empty cardboard box and plucking it with a stiff cardboard plectrum. Demonstrate how to change the sound by pressing the band at various places along the box.

Make a traditional Spinning Drum

Children love these easy-to-make spinning drums – also known as the 'monkey drum'.

Decorate with pre-printed Japanese letters or cherry blossom designs – try making pink blossoms by dipping the end of a cotton bud in pink paint and using it to dab little circles of blossom on the drum. Use another cotton bud to make little green leaves for a lovely traditional, Japanese print.

You will need:

- A sturdy cardboard ring, like the sort found in the middle of a sticky tape roll, or use a large roll cut into rings

- A 6 inch long piece of dowel (or something similar)

- String

- 2 beads

- Sticking tape

- Glue

- Decorations – stickers/cut-outs/paints and cotton buds.

Method:

Make two holes in the wall of the cardboard ring – on opposite sides to each other, using a large nail, plus a hole for the dowel stick handle.

Decorate both the insides and outsides of the roll as you choose.

Thread a length of string through both the holes – long enough to wrap around to the front of the drum with the ends meeting.

Tie knots in the string on each side of the drum to secure firmly in place.

Tie a bead to each end of the string.

Cover both sides of the cardboard ring with clear tape, stretching the tape tightly to produce a good sound.

Add the handle.

Play the drum in the traditional way – by twirling the handle round in the palms of your hands so the beads hit the drum faces, making a rhythmic drumming sound.

This English translation of a traditional Japanese children's rhyme (doesn't rhyme so well in English) could be used to accompany a Kodomo no hi craft display:

**'Carp windsocks are above the roof.
The biggest carp is the father,
The smaller carp are children,
They're enjoying swimming in the sky.'**

Links to learning – EYFS Development Matters

The focus of this chapter is on both setting goals and achieving them through perseverance, and celebrating a child's personality, and introduces many craft activities to explore the traditional customs associated with Kodomo no Hi. It fits particularly well into the Expressive Arts and Design area of the curriculum.

(Looking specifically at the 40-60+months age group.)

Expressive Arts and Design – Exploring and Using Media and Materials

A Unique Child

Begins to build a repertoire of songs and dances.

Explores the different sounds of instruments.

Explores what happens when they mix colours.

Experiments to create different textures.

Understands that different media can be combined to create new effects. Manipulates materials to achieve a planned effect.

Constructs with a purpose in mind, using a variety of resources.

Uses simple tools and techniques competently and appropriately.

Selects appropriate resources and adapts work where necessary.

Selects tools and techniques needed to shape, assemble and join materials they are using.

Early Learning Goal

Children sing songs, make music and dance, and experiment with ways of changing them. They safely use and explore a variety of materials, tools and techniques, experimenting with colour, design, texture, form and function.

June: Duanwu Festival

Duanwu, also known as the **Dragon Boat Festival** and the Double Fifth, is a traditional holiday originating in China and is celebrated in a number of East Asian and Southeast Asian countries and dates back 2400 years.

It was originally held to commemorate the death of Qu Yuan – a patriotic Chinese poet and exiled minister in the State of Chu, who supported the decision to fight against the King and powerful State of Qin, one of the seven states involved in the Warring States Period (476 BC-221 BC). After Qu Yuan killed himself by drowning in the Miluo river, the local people would paddle out in boats as an act of remembrance. This, in time, developed into a national holiday with dragon boat races.

The festival is sometimes known as the Double Fifth as it is traditionally celebrated on May 5th according to the Chinese lunar/solar calendar – usually falling in June in the Gregorian calendar.

Dragon boats are long and narrow with a dragon head and tail which are often beautifully decorated. A team of paddlers follow the drumbeat of a large drum to work in unison to power the boat along.

The Dragon Boat Festival is now celebrated in many countries including England, the U.S. and Canada with traditional dragon boat races, while the Chinese people and those in neighbouring countries also observe various traditional customs specific to their region.

Among these customs are the wearing of a perfumed pouch around the neck, wrist or ankle, making and wearing a five-coloured silk thread bracelet, eating zongzi and hanging mugwort leaves and calamus plants.

Another Dragon Boat Day tradition, popular with children, involves trying to balance an egg on its end. It is said this will bring good luck in the coming year if carried out during

Hanging Mugwort leaves and Calamus

It is believed the aroma of Mugwort leaves and magical properties of Calamus plants help keep flies and mosquitoes away, discourage disease and purify the air, and small bunches of these plants are commonly hung over doorways during Duanwu for good luck.

Eating Zongzi

Zongzi (pyramid-shaped glutinous rice parcels wrapped in reed or bamboo leaves) is the traditional food eaten during the Dragon Boat Festival. It can be made with various fillings which include: jujube (small date-like fruit), sweetened bean paste, meat or egg yolk.

Row, row, row your boat

This old favourite is lots of fun and also makes a great warm-up activity for drama or P.E. lessons. It's also a nice, simple activity to use as part of a class assembly on the dragon boat festival.

Start by putting children into teams of five or six. Then get everyone to climb into their imaginary boat – children sitting in a line, all facing the same way. Pick up the oars and all row together while you sing the rhyme. You can have a child banging the rhythm on a drum to keep everyone rowing in time like the drummer in a dragon boat.

Alternatively, have children sit in pairs, facing each other and holding hands. Children can rock back and forth as if rowing a boat along the river as they sing, making sure everyone watches out for the crocodiles (don't forget to scream), the polar bears (don't forget to shiver) and lions (don't forget to roar).

Row, row, row your boat

Row, row, row your boat
Gently down the stream
Merrily, merrily, merrily, merrily
Life is but a dream

Row, row, row your boat
Gently down the stream
If you see a crocodile
Don't forget to scream

Row, row, row your boat
Gently down the river
If you see a polar bear
Don't forget to shiver

the hours of 11am and 1pm; known as horse hour in Chinese astrology – the Dragon Boat Festival itself usually falls within the Chinese month of the horse (June).

Customs

Perfume pouches

It is traditional during Duanwu for children to wear small perfumed pouches, which according to folklore, will help protect them from evil. The pouches are made of colourful silk cloth and are strung together with red, yellow, blue, white and black thread and traditionally contain fragrant herbs.

Five-colour-thread bracelet

In China, the tying of five colours of silk thread holds special significance in that it is believed to contain magical and healing powers. It is customary for adults to tie the bracelets around children's wrists – sometimes neck or ankles, while children keep completely silent throughout. Children are not permitted to remove their silk threads until the first summer rainfall, when they remove their threads and throw them into the river. This is believed to protect them from plague and disease. (See **Make it!** section, page 42.)

Row, row, row your boat
Gently to the shore
If you see a grumpy lion
Don't forget to roar.

Dragon Boat Festival assembly piece

This simple story tells of the traditions still followed by many families to bring luck and good health, and to mark this special day.

Use as an assembly piece with teacher narrating the part of the mum and a child from your group taking the part of the little boy, Han. It really doesn't matter if the child (Han) can only remember a word of two of the script, as you can read with him – just make it fun. Other children in your group can join in by showing their hand-made traditional good luck Duanwu crafts, and you can also have children playing Chinese music at the beginning and end of the assembly – tambourines, bell sticks, little hand drums, xylophones and

Han's Dragon Boat Festival Day

It was the morning of the Dragon Boat Festival and Han woke up to find his mother carrying a large bunch of leaves.

Han walks in yawning

Han: Good morning mum. Why are you carrying all those leaves?

Mum: Good morning Han. These leaves are to decorate our house on this special day – the Duanwu Festival. These leaves are from special plants called Mugwort and Calamus, and we like to think the special smell of these plants will keep pesky mosquitoes and flies away from our house, and they will also keep our house smelling nice and fresh.

Mum hangs the leaves up and picks up her threads

Mum: And we also use these five silk threads in red, yellow, blue, white and black, to bring us luck on this special day. These special colours will protect you and bring you good luck.

Mum ties the coloured threads round Han's wrist

Mum: You should wear this bracelet until it rains, then you should throw it into a river and watch it float away like a five coloured dragon, and, you are supposed to stay quiet – no talking – until the bracelet is tied in place.

Han: Thanks for the bracelet mum, but is breakfast nearly ready – I'm starving!

triangles all make a lovely Chinese sound. You could finish with a chorus of row, row, row your boat (see opposite) for a bit of extra fun.

Make it!

Making a perfume pouch

These little perfumed bags make lovely gifts.

If making them in June to coincide with Duanwu, they could also make a nice Father's Day gift – just add 5 drops of aftershave to the rice instead of lavender and the bags can be hung in a wardrobe to keep clothes smelling lovely.

You will need (per pouch):

● 1 circular piece of cloth (about the size of a saucer) Felt is probably easiest to work with

Mum: Yes Han, breakfast is ready, and because today is a special Day we have rice dumplings wrapped in bamboo leaves, called Zongzi.

Han: They sound delicious Mum, and can we watch the dragon boat races later?

Mum: Yes we can. I love to see the big boats with their beautiful carved dragon heads and bright colours.

Han: When I grow up, I want to be the man who sits in the boat beating the big drum.

Mum: That would be so exciting Han. It must be lots of fun to be in a dragon boat race, and the drummer's job is very important – he beats the drum to help all the rowers keep time together. Oh! I nearly forgot one last thing – your special little perfume bag.

Han: What is a perfume bag Mum?

Mum: It's a special little bag made of brightly coloured cloth, containing sweet smelling Chinese herbs. We wear them because mosquitos and bugs don't like the smell, so they stay away and don't bite us. We like to give these little bags to the people we love.

Mum puts the bag round Han's neck.

Han: Thanks mum – Happy Duanwu!

Mum: Happy Duanwu, Han.

- Large needle and thread

- Approximately 1 tablespoon of dry rice

- Funnel (or make one from paper)

- Five drops of lavender essential oil or aftershave

- Small lump of cotton wool

- Scissors.

Method:

(This is an activity to use with small groups as sewing is tricky.)

Help children draw a circle on a piece of cloth – letting them choose the colour if possible, and cut out.

Help children sew nearly all the way round their circle, being careful not to leave big gaps.

Gently pull thread to gather into a pouch.

Leave needle and thread hanging while you stuff bag with a little cotton wool. Then use a funnel to help you add rice.

Carefully add five drops of lavender oil or aftershave to the rice – which holds the scent really well.

Sew up the opening, pulling thread further to give a gathered effect before fastening off. You might like to decorate with a little bow, by tying a length of ribbon around the top of the pouch.

These little bags are traditionally worn around the neck or pinned to clothing – pinning to clothes being safer with young children.

Making a five-coloured-thread bracelet

This is probably the easiest way ever to make a five-colour-thread bracelet, so perfect for pre-schoolers who can each make a few.

You will need:

- Five lengths of wool/embroidery thread per bracelet, one length each of red, blue, yellow, black and white.

Method:

Tie the five lengths of wool together at one end and twist together. Tie around the wrist or ankle.

Tell children not to talk while you tie the bracelet, as is the custom.

Have a mini Dragon Boat race

This is a great activity for a sunny day, when you can use a small paddling pool to race the boats

You will need (per boat):

- 1 plastic tray – from food packaging

- 1 lolly stick

- Red paper for making flag

- 4 little gold stars plus 1 larger gold star

- Sticky tape.

Method:

First make your flags (sails). It's a nice idea to make traditional Chinese flags for your boats and all you need is red paper, 4 little gold stars plus 1 larger star.

You could make dragon flags if you prefer, and older children especially, might prefer to create their own dragon design.

Fix flags securely to lolly sticks with sticky tape, then fix flags upright in the middle of boats with a blob of blue tack or plasticine.

Some larger dragon boats display ceremonial umbrellas as part of their decoration, and if you can find some of those little cocktail umbrellas, they do make a lovely addition to the boats, especially as they are often decorated with Chinese style patterns – just fix in place with a little bit of blue tack or plasticine.

Now simply take your boat to a small paddling pool or water play trough, blow into the sail and see whose boat makes it across the pool first.

Links to learning – EYFS Development Matters

This chapter primarily focuses on a child learning about customs and traditions associated with a cultural festival important to his family. It fits particularly well into the areas of Understanding the World and Communication and Language.

(Looking specifically at the 40-60+ months age group.)

Understanding the World – People and Communities

A Unique Child

Enjoys joining in with family customs and routines.

Early Learning Goal

Children talk about past and present events in their own lives and in the lives of family members.

They know that other children don't always enjoy the same things, and are sensitive to this.

They know about similarities and differences between themselves and others, and among families, communities and traditions.

Communication and Language – Understanding

A Unique Child

Responds to instructions involving a two-part sequence.

Understands humour, e.g. nonsense rhymes, jokes.

Able to follow a story without pictures or props.

Listens and responds to ideas expressed by others in conversation or discussion.

Early Learning Goal

Children follow instructions involving several ideas or actions.

They answer 'how' and 'why' questions about their experiences and in response to stories or events.

July: Ratha Yatra Festival

Ratha Yatra – meaning 'chariot journey' is an annual Hindu festival held during India's rainy season – the months of June and July. It is held on the second day of Shukla pakshya (waxing cycle of the moon) of Ashadh Maas (third month in the lunar calendar).

The festival is a very special event in the Eastern part of India, particularly in Puri, in the state of Orissa, and is held in honour of Lord Jagannath (Lord of the Universe). Jagannath is a form of Krishna

In Puri there is a large Jagannath Temple, which houses wooden images of Lord Jagannath, his brother Balaram or Balabhadra, and sister Subhadra. The temple was built nearly eight centuries ago and is one of the four major traditional centres of pilgrimage in India. Although Hindus make pilgrimages to Jagannath temple all year round, it is considered to be very special if the pilgrimage is made during Ratha Yatra.

The festival attracts thousands of pilgrims from all parts of India, with the highlight of the day being the **chariot procession**, when three ornately decorated chariots, made to look like temples are pulled through the streets of Puri by thousands of devotees. Images of the three deities – Jagannath, Balaram and Subhadra each sit in their own chariot.

The journey commemorates the annual journey of Lord Jagannath, Lord Balabhadra and their sister Subhadra to the Gundicha temple (an important sanctuary of Lord Jagannath). On their return from the Gundicha Temple the three deities stop for a while near the Mausi Maa Temple (aunt's house) and receive an offering of Poda Pitha (special type of pancake) believed to be the Lord's favourite. After a stay of seven days, the deities return to their home.

The huge procession accompanying the chariots sings devotional songs, accompanied by instruments such as drums, tambourines and trumpets. Children line the streets to see the procession and add to the chorus.

The chariots themselves, which are built anew every year, are huge – approximately 45 feet (14m) high are made from wood of specified trees and are constructed and colourfully decorated to traditional standards followed for centuries.

The festivals of Chandan Yatra and Snana Yatra directly precede Ratha Yatra and are integral parts of the celebration, each holding specific significance to the festival.

Chandan Yatra – The Sandalwood Festival

The construction of the three chariots always begins on what is known as Akshaya Trutiya – the third day of the bright fortnight of Vaisakha (April-May). This day marks the start of the new agricultural season when farmers will start ploughing their fields. The day also marks the beginning of what is known as the Summer Festival of the Deities, or the Sandalwood Festival, and lasts for three weeks.

During this time images of the deities are taken on a ceremonial boat ride everyday in a lake known as the Narendra Tank. They are finally given a ritual bath in a small temple in the middle of the lake in stone tubs containing water, sandalwood paste, flowers and perfumes. The rituals culminate in the Snana Yatra – Bathing Festival.

Snana Yatra – Bathing Festival

Held on the day of the full moon in the month of Jestha (May-June), Snana Yatra marks the taking of the three deities to a bathing platform – Snana Badi. The deities are then ceremonially washed with one hundred and eight pitchers of water brought from Suna Kua – the Golden Well. The deities then rest for about two weeks, during which time they are kept from public view and offered natural food stuffs in an act of convalescence.

An International Festival

The Ratha Yatra festival has now become an established celebration in many major cities throughout the world, including London, Melbourne, Venice, Toronto, Paris and New York.

The deities are unusual in that they are left unfinished. The hands are not properly formed, and the lower parts of their bodies are incomplete, the reason for this is explained in the following well-known legend.

Legend of the three statues

Long ago, a king named Indradyumna wished for someone to carve him special deity forms of Lord Krishna, his brother Balabhadra and sister Subhadra. An artist from the heavens known as Visvakarma, agreed to make these deities on the condition that no one would interrupt his work. King Indradyumna agreed to this and Visvakarma started carving the deities from within a locked room.

One day the king became so impatient to see the craftsman's work, he entered the room, but as soon as he did so, Visvakarma instantly vanished, leaving three unfinished carved forms. King Indradyumna was however, delighted, and placed the unfinished deities in a magnificent temple and worshipped them with great enthusiasm. Every year he arranged a great procession, during which, each of the deities rode on a beautifully decorated cart

Note: The following activities, although tying-in with the story of Ratha Yatra through their theme of statues and models, are not to be confused with the making of representations of Gods or idols in any respect, as this could prove disrespectful with many parents on religious grounds.

Watering my garden

Children love the challenge of staying completely still, and the following drama activities, which I have used many times in drama classes, have always proved popular. Also, try playing a game of musical statues as a good warm-up activity.

You will need:

- Atmospheric music such as 'Aquarium' from The Carnival of the Animals by Saint Saens or Bach's The Phantom of the Opera Theme

- Hall or suitable large space.

Method:

This game is great for encouraging imagination and playful movement. Before you begin, recap what has been learnt about the meaning of the word 'statue' and also explain the role of a gardener.

All children find a space – demonstrate how to turn around in a circle with arms outstretched, making sure you have plenty of room around you. Tell children you are a lady watering the plants in her garden, and they will be the beautiful flowers she is going to water. Show children how you will walk around the room pretending to water your plants. Children must stay perfectly still while you are near them and can see them, but, as soon as your back is turned, they can start to move. They must stay rooted to their spot,

but can change their position in any way they wish. When you catch a plant moving they are out. Last five plants left, win the game. Try adding some lovely music to garden to.

Children who are out can still join in being statues at the side of the hall – seeing who can make the best statue pose. Try giving them a 'statue pose challenge' to be working on, such as, practise making your best tree, ballet dancer or footballer.

Mr Freeze

A really good, fun game.

You will need:

- Twinkly music.

Ask all children to find themselves a space.

Method:

Tell children you are going to be 'Mr Freeze', a super hero with the power to turn everyone into ice just by touching them. Then children simply move about the room to music, while you creep among them – looking as menacing as you can. As soon as you touch a child they must freeze in a frozen position – spiky fingers, pointy elbows and toes and a surprised face. When all children are frozen, tell them to start melting, slowly, until they are just a puddle of water on the floor.

Alternative:

Tell them that they are to imagine they are a particular type of frozen food, frozen stiff in a freezer; the type of food is up to them. Some suggestions could be: A fish finger, sticky pudding or ice lolly. Once everyone has chosen their food, announce and mime that you are turning the freezer off. Now children must slowly defrost as they imagine their particular food would do – slowly getting soft and limp and eventually melting in a puddle on the floor.

A mime activity

The following mime activity can be incorporated into a Ratha Yatra assembly – or use with your group, just for fun.

Start by reading children the legend of the three statues, asking if children have seen statues before and show some pictures of examples – the Statue of Liberty, Nelson's Column, the Statue of Eros, The Angel of the North and any examples found in your group's local parks or town centre.

Next, put children in pairs – a sculptor and a block of wood. Tell children that the sculptor is to make a lovely statue by

Alyssa has used various materials to create her work. She described the materials "glitter, pom-poms. She said "a birdie and a nest".

pretending to carve the wood, and by carefully moving their partner's arms and hands into the desired position, but, listen carefully, because as soon as the music is turned off, the sculptor must immediately stop carving and everyone must freeze their position, while you inspect the work completed. Then pairs swap over roles of sculptor and statue. Some good music to use with this activity is Tchaikovsky's, The Nutcracker Suite.

Make it!

Junk modelling

Always a favourite, this is a hard activity to beat for creative possibilities, and brilliant for working on problem solving abilities as so much of it involves size, dimension, angles, and, just how can you make it all stick together? Rather than set a theme, just let children use their imaginations to create models of anything they wish. You can make the activity a bit special by focusing on the tactile aspect of junk modelling; supplying materials such as:

- Bubble wrap

- Balloons

- Old CDs

- Spare rolls of wallpaper

- Bottle tops

- Old clothes for cutting up

- Wrapping paper

- Foam washing up sponges

- Balls of wall/string

- Tin foil

- Corrugated card

- Nuts and bolts, nails, screws

- Disposable cups, spoons and forks and paper plates.

Sticky tape in tape dispensers is generally better than glue for sticking bits together, and gives instant results with no waiting for bits to dry. PVA glue will still be needed though, for fixing some materials together. Some other good fixing materials and apparatus to include could be:

- Rubber bands

- Pipe cleaners

Edible sparklers

Fireworks are an important part in many Ratha Yatra festivals, and these very easy to make edible sparklers are a fun way to introduce some of that festival excitement to young children.

You will need:

- Chocolate finger biscuits

- Small bowl of hundreds and thousands

- Small bowl of warm water

- Greaseproof paper.

Method:

These really couldn't be easier. All you have to do is dip one end of the biscuit finger into the warm water, then into the hundreds and thousands. Place on the greaseproof paper to set. Try alternatives to hundreds and thousands, such as desiccated coconut, sugar sparkles and edible glitter.

- Clothes pegs

- Split pins

- Hole punch

- Sticky dots and sticky foam pads

- Pinking scissors.

Also, you can make great use of lots of natural outdoors materials, and if you organise a treasure hunt, children can help find their own bits and pieces, such as: pine cones, twigs, dry leaves, pebbles and feathers. Just make sure everyone washes their hands at the end of the activity.

Junk modelling tips

- Try unsticking cardboard cereal boxes and turning inside out to give a plain box ready for decorating – really good for model buildings

- If you have the room, don't be afraid to go big. Big boxes children can sit in are brilliant for imaginative play, with children using them as cars, boats, houses, dog kennels…

- Models do not necessarily represent a recognisable object; abstract shapes and designs can be very effective too. Try showing children pictures of abstract sculptures and models, or better still, if you have anything like this near your setting, take children to see it themselves to get them thinking outside the box – so to speak!

- Be on hand to offer help with fixing things together as needed, there's no need to have children struggling – it's just too frustrating for children in this age group.

- Do offer ideas to children who get stuck for inspiration. Often it just takes a tiny suggestion from you to get their brains ticking over, and, show loads of enthusiasm for the work they produce – nothing goes on to inspire children – and adults – like a bit of praise.

Paint-blob firework picture

Staying with the fireworks theme, try these blow-paint firework pictures, which are particularly good saved for a sunny day outside when they will dry quickly and not cause too much mess.

You will need:

- 1 sheet of paper per child – A3 if possible
- Little dishes of quite watery paint in various colours
- A few drinking straws
- Teaspoon.

Method:

Use the spoon to put a little dollop of paint on the paper, and using a drinking straw, demonstrate how to gently blow to give a feathery, sparky effect.

Try adding a bit of extra sparkle by sprinkling some glitter over the paint while still wet. Also, try using black paper and lots of white and bright coloured or fluorescent paints to give a great night time effect.

Experiment with a bit of splatter painting too, especially effective with white paint on black paper as it creates the look of a beautiful starry night.

Links to learning – EYFS Development Matters

The main focus of this chapter is on movement – using controlled movements to create a storyline and fine motor movements during craft activities such as clay modelling. It covers the areas of physical development as shown opposite.

(Looking specifically at the 40-60+ months age group.)

Physical Development – Moving and Handling

A Unique Child

Experiments with different ways of moving.

Jumps off an object and lands appropriately.

Negotiates space successfully when playing racing and chasing games with other children, adjusting speed or changing direction to avoid obstacles.

Travels with confidence and skill around, under, over and through balancing and climbing equipment.

Shows increasing control over an object in pushing, patting, throwing, catching or kicking it.

Uses simple tools to effect changes to materials.

Handles tools, objects, construction and malleable materials safely and with increasing control.

Shows a preference for a dominant hand.

Begins to use anticlockwise movement and retrace vertical lines.

Begins to form recognisable letters.

Uses a pencil and holds it effectively to form recognisable letters, most of which are correctly formed.

Early Learning Goal

Children show good control and coordination in large and small movements.

They move confidently in a range of ways, safely negotiating space.

They handle equipment and tools effectively, including pencils for writing.

August: Ramadan

Ramadan is the name of the ninth month of the Islamic (lunar) calendar, and lasts 29-30 days.

During Ramadan, Muslims fast during daylight hours and it is a time of self-control, spiritual reflection, self-improvement, and increased worship, with extra thought given to the teachings of Islam.

Most Muslims will try hard to give up what they consider to be bad habits during Ramadan, which is chiefly achieved through prayer and reading the **Qur'an** (Holy book of Islam).

Fasting is of major importance during Ramadan and obligatory for most adult Muslims. It is intended to teach self-discipline, restraint and generosity, as well as acting as a reminder of the poor who often go without food.

During this time of fasting it is usual to have one meal – the suhoor, just before sunrise and another – the iftar, just after sunset. The period of fasting is often broken by Muslim friends and family joining together to share an evening meal in an act of friendly union.

Ramadan is considered especially important because it is said the Qur'an was first revealed to the Prophet Muhammad during this month. Muslims often attempt to recite as much of the Qur'an as they can during Ramadan, often being recited each night during Taraweeh prayers. It is also said to be a time when the gates of Heaven are opened, the gates of Hell closed, and all devils are chained up.

Taraweeh Prayers

These are long night prayers offered during Ramadan which, although not compulsory, are recommended and widely practised.

The Five Pillars of Islam

All Muslims are obligated to practice the Five Pillars of Islam in order to live a true Muslim life. They are:

- **Shahadah** – Reciting the Muslim profession of faith

- **Salat** – Performing obligatory Muslim prayers five times each day

- **Zakat** – Paying an alms (charity) tax to benefit those in need

- **Sawm** – Fasting during Ramadan

- **Hajj** – Making a pilgrimage to Mecca at least once during your lifetime.

The crescent moon and star

The symbol of a crescent moon around a five-pointed star is today internationally recognised as an emblem for Islam. The moon plays a significant role in the Islamic calendar as every new month starts with the first sighting of the 'hilal' – new crescent moon. Also, the new moon – always growing into a full moon, has been said by some to signify Islam as a growing religion, with the five-pointed star representing the Five Pillars of Islam.

The crescent moon and star motif can be found on top of the dome or minaret of many mosques as well as a motif in the mosque's interior prayer halls. It also features on the flags of several Muslim countries.

Mosques at this time are filled with worshippers attending Taraweeh prayer sessions which often last between one and a half and two hours. During this time long sections of the Qur'an are read and usually divided into equal parts so that sections may be read on successive evenings, with the entire Qur'an being recited by the end of Ramadan.

I'tikaf

I'tikaf (to stay in one place) Refers to time spent praying and reading the Qur'an in seclusion during the last ten days of Ramadan. Some Muslims live in the mosque at this time, to dedicate themselves to worship and reflection.

Lailat al Qadr – Night of Power or Night of Destiny

Lailat al Qadr, (also known as Shab-e-Qadr) commemorates what is considered to be the most important date in the Islamic calendar.

It is believed to be the anniversary of the night the first verses of the Qur'an were revealed to the prophet Muhammad by God (Allah).

It is usually observed on one of the last ten days of Ramadan and is traditionally spent in study and prayer, with many Muslims spending the whole night praying or reciting the Qur'an.

Eid al-Fitr

Eid al-Fitr – literally the 'Festival of Breaking the Fast,' is an important religious holiday celebrated by Muslims all over the world. It marks and celebrates the end of Ramadan.

Eid al-Fitr (often shortened to Eid) falls on the first day of the month of Shawwal in the Islamic lunar calendar and is a day for Muslims around the world to show a common goal of unity. Eid al-Fitr is a time when Muslims dress in their finest clothes and attend special prayer sessions where a special Eid al-Fitr salat (Islamic prayer) is recited. Homes are decorated with lights and decorations, and Muslims give gifts, especially to children, while spending time with family and friends.

Although a generous spirit is of fundamental importance throughout Islam, it is of special significance during Eid al-Fitr, when Muslims are obligated to help the poor and make contributions to mosques. This is also a time for thanking Allah for giving you enough self-control to get through the previous month of fasting.

Ramadan cultural celebrations

Today, in some Muslim countries Ramadan is celebrated with lights and lanterns strung in public places such as city streets. Stars and crescents are also a popular decoration during Ramadan and can be seen in various places such as shopping centres as well as in the home.

Today in Western countries you can even buy Ramadan calendars, which like the familiar Christmas advent calendar, contain a little toy or sweet behind a numbered door, helping make Ramadan more accessible to children too young to fast.

Eid assembly

Keep the assembly simple. Over the weeks leading up to the assembly, teach children some songs and rhymes about the moon and stars which they can recite as a group for the assembly (see below).

'The Owl and the Pussy-Cat' is a long rhyme for such young children to learn, but a lovely one to read to your group.

Hey Diddle, Diddle

Hey diddle diddle, the cat and the fiddle,
The cow jumped over the moon,
The little dog laughed to see such fun
And the dish ran away with the spoon.

Star Light, Star Bright

Star light, star bright,
First star I see tonight,
I wish I may, I wish I might,
Have the wish I wish tonight.

The Man in the Moon

The man in the moon,
Looked out of the moon,
Looked out of the moon and said,
'It's time for all the children on Earth
To think about getting to bed!'

The Owl and the Pussy-Cat (Edward Lear)

The Owl and the Pussy-Cat went to sea
In a beautiful pea-green boat
They took some honey, and plenty of money
Wrapped up in a five-pound note.
The Owl looked up to the stars above,

A note on inclusion

Opinions are quite divided over the use of music and drama in schools in relation to how their inclusion sits with Islamic beliefs, but as a generalisation, although some Muslim parents will not want their children to sing songs which contradict their faith e.g. Christmas carols, ordinary rhymes and songs should not cause a problem. The same basic principal applies to dance and drama lessons, where normal role-play activities should be acceptable.

Contention in this area usually only arises if it is felt alternative religious beliefs are being presented in a more favourable light than Islam. If parents appear apprehensive concerning lesson content, ask if they would like to sit in on a lesson and this should hopefully alleviate any concerns.

With regard to the assembly ideas on this page, it might be a good idea to introduce the assembly as an introduction to the month of Ramadan by simply looking at the moon and stars as these are symbols of the Islamic faith, pointing out any accompanying work you may have done on being kind and helping others, as these are of extra significance during Ramadan. Also, do ask if any Muslim parents have any relevant objects you could share at the assembly, such as Eid lanterns or 'Eid Mubarak' celebration cards.

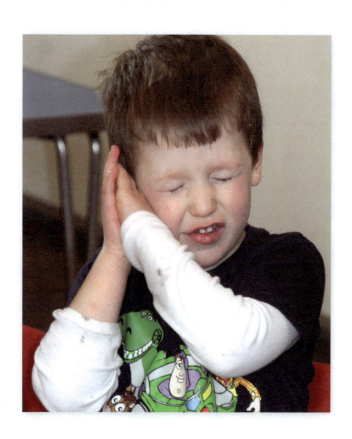

And sang to a small guitar,
"O lovely Pussy, O Pussy, my love,
What a beautiful Pussy you are,
You are,
You are!
What a beautiful Pussy you are!"

Puss said to the Owl, "You elegant fowl,
How charmingly sweet you sing!
Oh! let us be married; too long we have tarried,
But what shall we do for a ring?"
They sailed away, for a year and a day,
To the land where the bong-tree grows;
And there in a wood a Piggy-wig stood,
With a ring at the end of his nose,
His nose,
His nose,
With a ring at the end of his nose.

Dear Pig, are you willing to sell for one shilling
Your ring?" Said the Piggy, "I will."
So they took it away, and were married next day
By the turkey who lives on the hill.
They dined on mince and slices of quince,
Which they ate with a runcible spoon;
And hand in hand, on the edge of the sand,
They danced by the light of the Moon,
The Moon,
The Moon,
They danced by the light of the Moon.

Make it!

Phases of the Moon

The beginning of Ramadan is dependent on the sighting of the new crescent Moon because unlike the Western (Gregorian) calendar, the Islamic (Lunar) calendar is based on lunar patterns. The greatly anticipated announcement that the Ramadan Moon has been sighted is traditionally made by Islamic authorities throughout the world.

Try making some of the crafts shown below to show at your assembly.

Paper plate Moons

Although it would be nice to have a poster showing all the phases of the Moon for display, for this age group things will need to be kept simple with just new Moons, crescent Moons and full Moons which can be made and shown during assembly. Also, keep in mind that many pre-school children will have no knowledge of the changing appearance of the Moon and will only have

previously thought of it as a round shape. Do take time to explain that it constantly changes its appearance. An easy explanation is:

'The Moon is always moving round our planet; planet Earth. As it moves round, the Sun shines on different parts of the Moon, so sometimes it looks like it's changed shape.'

You will need (per child):

● 1 paper plate

● Black paint.

Method:

Let children pick which type of Moon they would like to make – have some examples ready-made. Using the black paint, let children create either a new Moon – paint the whole plate black (new Moons are not visible to us on Earth as the side of the Moon facing us is not lit by the sun), a crescent Moon – draw the crescent shape for them to paint around, or a full Moon – draw a circle in the middle of the plate for painting around. Don't worry if you end up with lots of some Moons and few of another – It's nice to let children choose.

Henna hands

Many Muslim women have their hands decorated with henna (powdered leaves of a tropical shrub, used as a dye) as part of their Eid celebrations. These henna designs are often very intricate and 'henna tattooing' has become quite an art form.

If you can find a mum with henna tattoos willing to show then to your children, this would be great, if not print some pictures from the internet and let children use these as inspiration.

You will need:

● A 4 paper

● Thin brown felt tip pens

● Scissors.

Method:

Have some simple pre-decorated hands pre-drawn and printed out so children can simply trace over the patterns with brown felt tipped pen. Follow on by drawing around children's hands to give two hand shapes, letting children decorate their own hand outlines with brown felt tipped pen to their design. Hands can be cut out for display.

Write a good deed note

During Ramadan, Muslims spend a lot of time thinking about being kind to others. During a circle time session, have children think about ways they might be able to help a friend or family member. Maybe they could offer to help mum with the housework, or tidy their bedroom really well. Have every child think of one good deed they could do for someone else and make a note of it on a small piece of paper, together with the child's name. Pin all the good deed notes on a display board. When children can tell you they've done their good deed, stick a gold star on their piece of paper under their name.

Make an Eid lantern

Lanterns are widely used during Eid as decorations to light up buildings and homes. These lanterns look lovely and are really simple to make. Collect little glass jars in the weeks leading up the activity so you have enough for everyone, alternatively, ask parents to donate one per child.

You will need:

- 1 glass jar per lantern

- PVA glue

- Coloured sequins, glitter and sparkly shapes

- 1 tea light per lantern.

Make some traditional Eid treats

Two very simple recipes to try with your group.

Traditional Eid sweets

You will need (makes approximately 20 sweets):

- 226g (8oz) icing sugar

- 5 tablespoons of condensed milk

- Few drops flavouring e.g. vanilla

- Few drops colouring (optional).

Method:

Mix all ingredients together to form a fairly stiff dough.

Give each child a small lump of the mixture, which can be either rolled and squashed into little sweets, or rolled and cut into star or moon shapes.

Sweets can also be sprinkled with hundreds and thousands.

Eid cookies

You will need (makes approximately 18):

- 100g (4oz) butter, softened

- 50g (2oz) caster sugar

- 150g (5oz) plain flour sifted

- A few drops vanilla flavouring.

Method:

Place softened butter and caster sugar in a bowl and beat until well creamed together.

Stir in the sifted plain flour and add vanilla flavouring, then mix to form a stiff dough. Wrap in cling film and cool for thirty minutes.

Preheat oven to 180°C, 350°F (gas mark 4).

Place dough on a lightly floured surface and roll out.

Cut out moon and star shapes and place on a lightly greased baking sheet and bake for 12-14 mins until a pale golden colour. Cool on a wire rack.

Method:

Make sure all jars have labels removed and are clean and dry, and then just let children decorate to their own design by gluing sequins onto their jar. Finish by adding a tea light.

Links to learning – EYFS Development Matters

Although this chapter covers many areas of the curriculum, it has a strong 'time' theme running through it; Ramadan being celebrated over the period of a month – a long time for young children. The chapter also contains various activities using shapes and patterns – both 2D and 3D, all of which fit nicely in the curriculum areas as shown below.

(Looking specifically at the 40-60+ months age group.)

Mathematics – Shape, Space and Measure

A Unique child

Beginning to use mathematical names for 'solid' 3D shapes and 'flat' 2D shapes, and mathematical terms to describe shapes.

Selects a particular named shape.

Can describe their relative position such as 'behind' or 'next to'.

Orders two or three items by length or height.
Uses familiar objects and common shapes to create and recreate patterns and build models.

Uses everyday language related to time.

Orders and sequences familiar events.

Measures short periods of time in simple ways.

Early Learning Goal

Children use everyday language to talk about size, weight, capacity, position, distance, time and money to compare quantities and objects and to solve problems.

They recognise, create and describe patterns they explore characteristics of everyday objects and shapes and use mathematical language to describe them.

September: Harvest Festival and Sukkot

Harvest Festival

Harvest Festivals – giving thanks for a bountiful harvest, are celebrated in various ways across the world, America's Thanksgiving national holiday being one example.

In Britain, people have given thanks for a good harvest since pagan times. Many old Harvest customs – singing hymns, decorating churches with crops and loaves of bread are still observed today.

In Britain, harvest celebrations are traditionally held on the Sunday nearest to the Harvest Moon – the full moon occurring closest to the Autumn Equinox, during September or early October.

During pagan times, agricultural communities would hold a huge harvest feast to mark the occasion. This harvest supper was presided over by the Lord of the Harvest, who would have been a well-regarded member of the community and who would take responsibility for carving the main dish of the day – roast goose. Although today this tradition is not usually observed, Goose Fairs are still held at harvest time in some rural communities, with fairground rides, cattle shows and food stalls.

Another well-known harvest custom is the making of corn dollies, which were used to decorate houses during the festival. Corn dollies (straw work decorations) were traditionally made from the last sheaf of corn cut, and were made in honour of the corn spirit, which in pagan times was believed to protect crops and have the power to guarantee a plentiful harvest the following year.

Corn dollies, traditionally being hollow structures, were originally thought to make a suitable home for the corn spirit who, usually living among the cereal crops, found herself homeless once the crops were harvested. The corn spirit could live in the corn dollie until spring came again, when it would be ploughed into the first furrow of the new season.

Sukkot

Sukkot, also known as the Feast of Booths or the Feast of Tabernacles, is a seven-day Jewish harvest holiday celebrated during the Hebrew month of Tishrei (varying between late September – late October). It starts four days after Yom Kippur and is followed by Shmini Atzeret and Simchat Torah.

Sukkot celebrations can be traced back to ancient Israel when the Jewish people would build huts near the edge of fields during the harvest season. A sukkah (sukkot being the plural) is a Hebrew word for these huts, which would provide shade and somewhere to stay during harvest time.

Sukkot is also connected to the biblical story of the Jewish people wandering the desert for forty years. Along their travels they would build tents or simple dwellings – sukkot, for shelter. Today the Sukkot holiday celebrates both Israel's agricultural history and the Jew's exodus from Egypt.

There are three major traditions associated with Sukkot, which are: building a sukkah, eating in a sukkah and waving the lulav and etrog.

The sukkah

Today, many Jewish people build a sukkah in their backyard or garden, or help construct one in a synagogue (Jewish place of worship). It is customary for the sukkah to be topped with branches and is often well decorated with harvest or Judaic themes, while the structure itself will be of a temporary nature and only used for the period of Sukkot. Few people will actually live in their sukkah, but many will have at least one meal in it, before which a special blessing will be recited – 'Blessed are you, Adonai our God, ruler of the universe, who has sanctified us with commandments, and commanded us to dwell in the sukkah.'

The Four Species

An important tradition related to Sukkot involves what is known as the Four Species, or, the Lulav and Etrog. It is

customary during Sukkot to take an etrog (citrus fruit native to Israel), a palm branch (lulav in Hebrew) a myrtle branch (hadas) and a willow branch (arava), and every morning during Sukkot, except on Shabbat (primarily a day of rest and spiritual enrichment, traditionally observed from a few minutes before sunset on Friday evening until the sighting of three stars in the sky on Saturday night). And take these branches (lulav) in the right hand and the etrog in the left, bringing them together with the stem of the etrog pointing downwards whilst reciting the following blessing: 'Blessed are you, our God, creator of time and space, who enriches our lives with holiness, commanding us to take the lulav and etrog.' The waving of the four plants is a 'mitzvah' (commandment) of the Torah (primary document of Judaism), and symbolises a Jew's service to God.

Harvest display: what fruit am I?

There are so many interesting and colourful fruits and vegetables available in the shops, and lots will be new to young children. Just pick a few of the most interesting looking varieties for showing to your group. Ask if anyone knows the name of each fruit or vegetable as it's shown, and tell your class which country they come from. If possible, let children taste the fruit, asking if they liked it or not. Use any remaining fruits or vegetables as part of a harvest display. Also, give children the chance to touch the fruits and vegetables – all the lovely shapes and textures of their skins; so different from the fruit inside.

Johnny Appleseed

Johnny Appleseed, whose real name was Jonathan Chapman (September 26th 1774 – March 18th 1845), was an American nurseryman responsible for introducing apple trees to large parts of America.

Legend has it, his dream was to plant so many apple trees that no one would ever go hungry, and paints a picture of Johnny as a wanderer, scattering apple seeds throughout the countryside. Research has shown though, that Johnny was actually an astute businessman, who managed to buy and sell many plots of land, planting thousands of apple trees which he sold very cheaply to American settlers – if they had no money though, they were given trees for free.

The following story of the life of Johnny Appleseed is a nice one to read to children at harvest time as it demonstrates how the planting of a seed goes on to bear more fruits and seeds in a never ending cycle. It also acts as a good introduction to the drama activity that follows.

Before reading the story talk about the meaning of the words nursery (in this context) and orchard, as these will probably be new to your children.

The story of Johnny Appleseed

This is the story of a real person who lived a long time ago in America and whose real name was John Chapman. John worked in a nursery, but not a nursery for looking after children; this was a plant nursery where little seeds are grown into plants. He loved planting seeds and growing plants and had the idea that if he planted lots and lots of apple seeds, these would grow into trees he could sell very cheaply to poor people who would then be able to sell their apples and get money to buy food.

So he slung a bag of apple seeds over his back and went exploring for spare land that didn't belong to anyone and started planting my seeds. First, he had to make sure he found a good piece of land for growing trees, then he would clear away all the weeds. Next he planted apple seeds in straight rows and built a fence around them using twigs and logs he found nearby, so wild animals wouldn't eat the little plants before they had a chance to grow.

Some people who came to live near the apple orchards gave him the name, 'Johnny Appleseed, and some called him the Apple Tree Man.

John spent a lot of time working all on his own, but he didn't mind because he loved being outside, seeing all the wild animals, insects and plants. He only charged a few pennies for each of his trees, but when some people had no money at all, he still let them have some trees because he was a very kind person.

Although Johnny lived a very simple life, he was very happy and made lots of friends along his travels. He didn't eat meat, so he gathered nuts and berries and sometimes his friends would give him milk from their cows or vegetables from their gardens. Sometimes friends would invite him to dinner, where he would have lots of exciting stories to tell them about his life living outdoors.

Johnny would get his apple seeds from places called cider presses, which were places where they squashed apples to get all the juice out to make a drink called apple cider – they didn't use the pips though, which was lucky for Johnny.

During his life, Johnny spent forty six years planting trees across America, and American people are very proud of him because he was such a kind man who worked very hard to help other people.

A little seed grows – a mime activity

This is a good little mime activity to use with young children as they can more or less create their own little drama.

Encourage children to use all their body and to really imagine they are a little seed getting bigger and stronger and growing tall, building a little story of their own. It also shows children that they can perform lots of movement without leaving their own little space.

Before starting the main activity, go through the meanings of the following words with your group to make sure everyone knows their meaning:

- Stem

- Bud

- Shoot

- Soil

- Seed.

Start by getting everyone sitting in their own space.

Show children how to stretch out their arms while turning around in a circle to make sure they have enough room.

A little seed grows: The Story

Start very quietly, so as not to wake the seeds

You are a little seed, fast asleep in the ground. It is winter time, and very cold and frosty, so you do not want to come out, you would rather sleep until it gets a bit warmer. You can't see anything at all, because it is completely dark under the ground.

One day, you start to feel a little bit warmer and you start to wake up. The ground around you feels wet because it's been raining and you have a little drink of water.

You want to see what's above the soil, so you slowly stretch up a little shoot. You stretch higher and higher and as you stretch upwards you feel warmer and warmer. You give one last, really big push, and burst through the soil!

The sun is shining brightly and it helps you grow taller and taller. It starts to rain and you have a big drink of water, and this helps you grow even taller.

One day a little bud starts to grow on one of your branches and it really tickles! At first it is just a tiny little bump, but then it grows into a (let children decide what type of fruit tree they would like to be). It gets bigger and bigger until one day, a little bird flies down, pecks off the fruit and flies away with it so he can eat it all up.

You feel very happy because you know some of the seeds from your fruit will fall back into the soil and grow into new plants – just like you!

Follow this activity with a circle time session about the activity above.

Reinforce important words, and ask questions such as:

- How do you think the little seed felt when it was under the ground?

- How do you think it felt once it came up through the ground and saw the world for the first time?

- Which fruit did you choose for your plant and why?

- Did you feel a little bit sad at first, when the bird flew down and pecked off your fruit?

- If you were a plant that grew beautiful flowers, what colour flowers would you like to grow?

Narrate the story while children act out the scene, leaving pauses so children have time to think about their movements and be a bit inventive.

Make it!

Grow a bean plant in a jar

You will need:

- A broad bean

- A saucer

- A glass jar

- Some paper towel

- Water.

Method:

Pre-soak the beans for about an hour for best results.

Put a little water in your jar and swirl about to get the sides of the jar wet. Roll up a couple of sheets of paper towel and stick to the inside of your jar. Place your bean between the paper towel and the side of your jar.

Stand on a sunny windowsill and water daily to keep paper moist – try using a spoon or water dropper to water your bean. You should see some little sprouts after about four days, and by ten days you should have a bean plant with leaves, a stem and lots of roots.

To grow plant on, you will need to plant your bean in a pot containing compost, and water frequently.

Children can keep a record of the beans progress by drawing a picture of its stage of growth every couple of days.

Make some play dough harvest loaves

A really easy craft activity that's lots of fun and fits in nicely with a harvest theme

Home-made play dough

You will need:

- 1 cup plain flour
- Half cup salt
- 1 tablespoon of oil
- 2 tablespoons cream of tartar
- 1 cup of water
- Rolling pin.

Method:

Mix all dry ingredients together, add water and mix together.

Transfer the mixture to a saucepan and cook on a medium heat, stirring constantly.

Allow to cool before giving it a bit of a knead until you have a good consistency.

Demonstrate how to make three long sections of dough and form a plait, although children may find it easier to make cottage loaf shapes by placing a small ball of dough on top of a larger one, or little bread rolls or French stick shapes.

You can sprinkle with sesame seeds or something similar if available.

Leave to dry.

Extend the learning by growing some cress seeds – always good for a growing topic as you get such quick results.

Links to learning – EYFS Development Matters

This chapter looks closely at habitats, environments and living things – especially plants. These areas are primarily covered in the area of Understanding the World, as shown below

(Looking specifically at the 40-60+ months age group.)

Understanding the World – The World

A Unique Child

Looks closely at similarities, differences, patterns and change.

Early Learning Goal

Children know about similarities and differences in relation to places, objects, materials and living things.

They talk about the features of their own immediate environment and how environments might vary from one another.

October: Diwali

Probably the most well-known of Hindu festivals, **Diwali** is a five day festival celebrated in India and other countries with a Hindu population. The name Diwali means 'rows of lighted lamps' and Diwali is often referred to as **'The Festival of Lights'**, as houses and public places are decorated with small earthenware oil lamps called Diyas.

The date of the festival is decided upon by the position of the moon. Amavasya, or 'no moon day' in the Hindu month of Kartik is considered to be the perfect day to celebrate Diwali, usually falling in November or December in the Western, Gregorian calendar.

Focusing on the awareness of 'inner light' is of major significance during Diwali, believing there is something more significant than the physical mind and body, which is pure, infinite and eternal, is a central Hindu philosophy. This inner light is called the 'Atman', a Sanskrit word meaning 'self'.

Diwali marks the end of the harvest season in most of India, and it's a time to give thanks for the harvest and pray for a good harvest in the coming year.

Traditionally, the old business year closes and the new business year starts at Diwali.

Blessings are bestowed upon Lakshmi, the Goddess of wealth and prosperity at this time too, and the lighting of the diya lamps is said to help Lakshmi find her way into people's homes so she may give her blessings to the family. Diwali is also a time for telling one of the Diwali legends, which tells of Rama and Sita's return to Rama's kingdom after fourteen years of exile.

Typical Diwali activities include: cleaning the house, wearing new clothes, making special foods and family meals, exchanging gifts, decorating homes and buildings with lights, and holding and visiting big firework displays.

Giving gifts

Diwali is a time for giving gifts to family, friends and loved ones. Traditionally dried fruits and sweets were given, but this has given way to a tendency to give more expensive gifts. Diwali is also traditionally a time to buy new clothes and redecorate the home.

Gambling

There is a well-known legend that explains the tradition of gambling at Diwali – as the goddess Parvati was playing dice with her husband, Lord Shiva, she decreed that anyone gambling on Diwali night would prosper throughout the coming year. Playing cards for money is very popular during Diwali and there is a saying that goes, 'one who does not gamble on this day will be reborn as a donkey in his next birth.' As you can imagine, casinos do very well during Diwali week.

Fireworks

Fireworks and firecrackers play an important part in the Diwali celebrations – lighting up the night as a symbol of light triumphing over darkness. In recent years though, there have been calls against them due to environmental issues, noise pollution and a number of accidental deaths and injuries.

Try some Indian dancing

As part of a PE lesson, try playing some traditional Indian music for children to dance to. If you have a parent – or if your setting is a school nursery, an older child in the school who practises traditional Indian dancing – encourage them to come along to show children how it should be done, and to teach them a couple of simple moves they could demonstrate at an assembly.

Have a Diwali assembly or sharing day

Diwali is a great theme for a special assembly or sharing day, as it has lots of little traditions that can be introduced. Try narrating this simple script while children introduce the various Diwali customs along the way. And, if you're lucky enough to have parents willing to bring in Dija lamps or other Diwali decorations, you can show these during your assembly too.

Make it!

Rangoli patterns

A rangoli is a colourful design traditionally made with the fingers using flour, coloured sand, chalk or rice. They are

The story of Rama and Sita

(Child-friendly version for reading to your group)

The following is one of several traditional stories related to Diwali.

Once upon a time there was terrible demon king called Ravana. He had ten heads and twenty arms and everyone was scared of him. He wanted to make a beautiful woman called Sita his wife, but she was already married to a great warrior prince named prince Rama.

One day Ravana tricked Sita by pretending to be an old man. He kidnapped Sita and took her away in his chariot, but Sita had a clever idea – she dropped all her jewellery along the way, so her husband, Rama, could follow the trail.

Rama saw the jewellery glittering and twinkling, and together with his brother, Lakshman, followed the trail.

On the way they met Hanuman, the monkey king who had wings and could fly, and they became friends. Hanuman said he would help Rama and Lakshman find Sita and he sent messages to all the monkeys in the world, and the monkeys told all the bears, and they all set out to find Sita.

They searched and searched for a very long time, then one day Hanuman, the monkey king, found Sita, she was imprisoned on Ravana's island. But how could all the monkeys and bears reach the island to rescue Sita? They had an idea, they would build a bridge, but they would need lots of help.

Soon, all the animals in the world, all the really big animals and all the really little animals, and all the middle sized animals came to help them build the bridge.

Once the bridge was finished, the animals raced across to the island and had a mighty battle with King Ravana that lasted ten days. It looked like King Ravana was going to win, but in the end, prince Rama, and his friends won, and people across the land celebrated.

As Prince Rama, Sita and their friends headed back home it was getting dark, so the villagers put little oil lamps called diyas in their windows to help them find their way – they looked like little twinkling stars shining in the night sky.

Diwali celebrations

Narrator: Welcome to our assembly. Today we are going to share with you some of the things we have been learning about Diwali. Diwali means, rows of lighted lamps, and is an important Hindu New Year festival that takes place around October and November. It is a festival that contains several customs, which we will show you in our assembly.

At Diwali time, many people give their home a really good clean to make it nice for the coming year. Hindus also hope the goddess Lakshmi will bless the family and house if it is nice and clean.

Children clean with their dustpans, brushes and dusters

Some Hindu ladies decorate their hands and feet with mendhi patterns, using a brown dye called henna, and families decorate their homes with colourful decorations during Diwali to celebrate the festival. This includes making special floor designs called rangoli, which are colourful patterns made from coloured sand, powder or rice, often made near the entrance to a house to welcome visitors. If the patterns are beautiful it is hoped Lakshmi, the goddess of wealth and prosperity will visit your home to bless you with good luck.

Children show their rangoli pictures

At Diwali, people also like to give each other greetings cards that wish a Happy Diwali.

Children show their Diwali cards

Diwali is a time for making and eating lots of lovely food and for sharing this with friends and family and sometimes taking sweets to friend's houses.

Children show some of the sweets they made

During Diwali special little oil lamps called diyas are used to light houses. They are made from clay and have cotton wicks dipped in oil.

Children show their diya lamps

Diwali is a very special time for Hindus, and all the family like to celebrate with music and dancing. Everyone gets together to have a really lovely time. This is the end of our Diwali assembly. I hope you have all enjoyed it. We have had lots of fun learning about Diwali.

Children dance to traditional Indian music to end assembly

Things to do

- Gather together the essential resources listed – making any changes to suit your own requirements along the way.

Essential resources

- Diwali crafts for showing to the audience – just a selection, with children showing one item each.

- Traditional Indian music to play as people are entering and leaving the hall.

- Little dustpans, brushes and dusters.

made to welcome the Goddess Lakshmi into the home, so made on the floor, usually near the entrance to a home.

There are many different designs of rangoli, but they are mostly symmetrical. The motif of the designs is often taken from nature, such as flowers or birds.

Before children make their own rangoli patterns, print some pictures of examples from the Internet so children can see how the real thing looks.

With such young children, it is probably best to print out your own simple patterns, so children only need to fill in the spaces with coloured chalks. Alternatively, you could let children make some of their own designs on fine sand paper. This is a good medium to use with chalk and also gives a feeling of chalking on the pavement.

Make a diya lamp

You will need (per child):

- A small piece of air drying clay or plastercine

- 1 tea light candle

- 1 tea light holder to use for moulding

- Glitter or sparkly shapes.

Method

Take the piece of clay or plastercine and give it a bit of a knead to make it more manageable, then mould into shape using the bottom of the tea light holder (or small cup).

Roll in glitter or sparkly shapes, giving a bit of a press to secure in place.

Leave to dry – if using clay, then finish off by adding a tea light candle.

Light a couple of the diya lamps to show children how lovely they look when lit – reinforce the safety aspect though, saying children must NEVER try to light anything, and this is always only done by adults.

Diwali cards

There are lots of different designs of Diwali cards available, but as Diwali is part Hindu harvest festival, it's a nice idea to incorporate the harvest theme into your greeting card activity by using natural materials such as pulses.

There are lots of highly colourful pulses available in the shops, just choose which ever ones catch your eye.

Pulses are also appropriate here as they are widely used in traditional Indian cuisine – India being the world's biggest producer and consumer of pulses.

No-cook barfi recipe

Try this really simple version of a traditional recipe widely eaten during Diwali.

Ingredients:

- 225g desiccated coconut
- 100g icing sugar
- 200g condensed milk

Method:

Mix all ingredients together in a large bowl.

Turn out onto work surface and roll into little balls.

Roll in icing sugar and refrigerate to set.

Keep two or three sweets in a refrigerator for showing at a Diwali assembly or sharing day.

You could also buy a small box of traditional, mixed Indian sweets for children to taste for an authentic taste of Diwali, or, if you have any parents willing to donate some of their home made Indian sweets, even better!

You will need (per child):

- 1 sheet A4 paper card folded in half
- A mixture of colourful pulses which are suitable for gluing on card – red, green and brown lentils are good as they're small and flat
- PVA glue and spreader
- Pre-printed Happy Diwali greeting for gluing to front of card.

Method

Glue the greeting to the front of the card first – while there's still room, then children can either simply make their own collage designs using the pulses, or you can have a rangoli or diya lamp design pre-drawn for children to work with, then leave to dry.

It's an idea to write children's names inside before decorating cards, to stop bits being knocked off, especially if children are going to write their own name.

Links to learning – EYFS Development Matters

There is quite a bit of movement going on in this chapter, with Diwali being a very joyful, colourful time, with dancing,

fireworks and lights at the forefront of the celebrations. The above activities fully cover the development areas covered by Expressive Arts and Design – Being Imaginative.

(Looking specifically at the 40-60+ months age group.)

Expressive Arts and Design – Being Imaginative

A Unique Child

Create simple representations of events, people and objects.

Initiates new combinations of movement and gesture in order to express and respond to feelings, ideas and experiences. Chooses particular colours to use for a purpose.

Introduces a storyline or narrative into their play.

Plays alongside other children who are engaged in the same theme.

Plays cooperatively as part of a group to develop and act out a narrative.

Early Learning Goal

Children use what they have learnt about media and materials in original ways, thinking about uses and purposes.

They represent their own ideas, thoughts and feelings through design and technology, art, music, dance, role play and stories.

November: Guru Nanak's Birthday

Guru Nanak (lived 1469-1539 under the Nanakshani calendar, his birthday usually falling in November in the Western calendar) was the first of the ten Sikh Gurus and the founder of the **Sikh** religion. Sikhs follow Guru Nanak's teachings and those of his followers, the nine Sikh Gurus.

His teachings were based on the principal of there being only one God who is accessible to all, without the need for priests or rituals and that everyone is equal.

This was in its time a controversial belief, as it was a denouncement of the caste system. The South Asian caste system is the traditional organising of society into a hierarchy of hereditary groups. It is fixed by birth and also associated with particular occupations. Marriage strictly remains within one's caste and is underpinned by traditional Hindu religious principles.

Guru Nanak

Born into a Hindu family, Guru Nanak himself did not take part in a ceremony of initiation into the Hindu religion saying he was neither Hindu nor Muslim. Guru Nanak worked for a Muslim as he grew up and gained useful insight into the Muslim faith.

He went on to become a religious teacher, teaching about his new faith which combined ideas from both Hinduism and Islam and which he called Sikhism.

Nanak travelled great distances spreading word of his new religion, writing hymns along the way, his most famous of which is the Jappi, which Sikhs recite each day at dawn. Before he died, Guru Nanak told Lehna – his most trusted follower, that he should be the next guru. Lehna became known as Guru Angad.

Three of Nanak's most important teachings are known as nam simran, kirt karo, and wand chako:

Nam Simran: Think about God.

Kirt Kaara: Live a simple life. Earn a living through honest means and hard work.

Wand Chhako: Share with the needy whatever you can spare. Treat all men and women as equals regardless of nationalities, religions or creed.

Guru Nanak believed and taught:

- There is only one God, who is accessible to all, and he alone should be worshipped
- Everyone is equal – man will be judged by his actions alone
- Empty religious rituals and superstitions have no value.

He believed people should:

- Live a simple, honest, good life, free from fear

- Work hard
- Help others, regardless of race, creed or social standing
- Show kindness to all living creatures and prey for the good of all.

How Guru Nanak's birthday is celebrated

Sikhs celebrate Guru Nanak's birthday as well as other Gurpurbs (festivals celebrating the lives of the Gurus) by reading the entire **Guru Granth Sahib** (Sikh Holy Book) over a two day period finishing on the morning of Guru Nanak's birthday. This is performed by a group of men and women, taking turns at reading for 2-3 hours each.

The day prior to Guru Nanak's birthday is a time for processions led by five people representing the original Panj Piare (Five Beloved Ones) accompanied by singers and musicians. Gurdwaras (meaning the gateway to the Guru, and the Sikh place of worship) are decorated with flowers and lights, and hymns from the Guru Granth Sahib are sung here as part of the celebrations.

The congregation will go on to share a meal from the free kitchen (langar), including the sweet treat, Karah Prashad, which is blessed. Celebrations may also include fireworks and martial arts displays.

Drama activities

The following activities have proved popular with groups I've taught in the past. They are nice ones to use when learning about Guru Nanak as he was known to be a great traveller. Demonstrate some ideas yourself to get children started – always a good idea with very young children.

Weather-walking warm-up

Everyone starts by walking around the room, reminding children they can use all four corners of the room and to not all bunch up in the middle – with this age group, it might be a good idea to have everyone walking in the same direction, to avoid bumping into one another.

Once everyone is walking about nicely, instruct children that the weather has become very windy. So windy, they can hardly walk. They are nearly getting blown over and have to button their coats and hold their hats on to stop them flying away. Show children how they might walk in very windy weather – head bowed down, with shoulders pushing forwards, finding it difficult to keep balanced.

Go on to introduce various other weather patterns, such as:

The North Wind and the Sun

The following activity based on a well-known fable, is a good one to follow on from the above. Reading through the story first makes things much easier as children know what's coming next. Finally read through, stopping at the highlighted sections, for children to act the part of the travelling man.

The North Wind was always showing off, saying how strong and powerful he was and telling the Sun he was much better than him.

"I am so strong and powerful, I can do anything I want," boasted the North Wind. "I am the greatest, and much better than you Mr Sun, all you do is shine on people and warm them up. But I can blow their umbrellas inside-out, I can blow their pants off the washing line – I can even blow the roofs off their houses if I feel like it. Oh yes, I am certainly stronger than you."

The Sun was getting a bit fed up with the North Wind's showing off and thought he would teach him a lesson, so he set him a challenge. "As you think you are so powerful and mighty, would you would like to have a little competition?" asked the Sun. "Take a look at the road below us, can you sees that man travelling along the path?" "Yes, I see him," said the North Wind.

"As a test of strength, let's see who can make him take his winter coat off. Whoever manages to do it will be the winner and will have proved that they are the strongest," said the Sun. "That's easy-peasy," boasted the North Wind. "I'll go first."

The North Wind started to blow. He blew quite gently at first, sending a little cloud of dust spinning in the air. But this didn't seem to bother the travelling man, who simply carried on his way. So the Wind blew a little harder, making the branches of trees sway, and blowing a few leaves to the ground. But the travelling man simply pulled his coat around him nice and close, to keep warm. This made the North Wind very angry, and so he blew very, very hard. He roared through the tree tops, blowing over a few trees, and sending so much dust and so many leaves flying about that the travelling man could hardly see where he was going. He buttoned up his coat all the way to the top and he put his hands in his pockets to keep them warm.

"Oh dear, Oh dear," said the Sun. "That didn't work at all. Let me see if I can do any better. It's my turn.

And the Sun started to shine. At first the travelling man became just a little bit warmer, and took his hands out of his pockets. Then he undid the top button of his coat, then he was so hot, he took his coat off altogether and carried it over his arm, enjoying the lovely warm weather. He even undid the top button of his shirt.

"I've won!" said the Sun. "I won by being gentle. You see, you're more likely to get what you want if you are nice and gentle, rather than all rough and tough."

"It was a silly challenge anyway," said the North Wind grumpily, and he blew himself away in a huff. The Sun smiled a big smile and knew the North Wind wouldn't be showing off ever again – and he didn't.

- A very hot day

- An icy day – very slippery

- A foggy day – difficult to see where you're walking

- Thunderstorm

- A snowy day – lots of opportunities for snowball fights and snowman building.

Go on to introduce other scenarios such as:

- Walking on the moon (demonstrate)

- A very busy street with lots of people getting in your way

- Climbing up a steep mountain

- Walking through thick sticky mud

- Walking with sticky bubblegum stuck to the bottom of your shoes

- Walking through a jungle – maybe there are dangerous creatures lurking in the bushes.

Make it!

Make some gift boxes

Sikhs believe they serve God by serving others, and many Sikhs carry out chores in the Gurdwara as part of their service to the community, often working in the Langar – free food kitchen, as a way of helping others. Sikhs also regard caring for the poor and sick as an important duty.

Talk to children about why it is important to help others, and ways we can all do this. Also thinking about people in the community who help us such as lollypop men and women, the police and fire services and adults in schools and nurseries.

You will need:

- A few empty shoe boxes

- Craft scrap box decoration materials

- Donations of food items – it is really nice if these could be largely more luxury items, such a chocolate, drinking chocolate, tea bags, biscuits and little cakes, but nothing too perishable.

Make your own Karah Prashad

**Makes approximately 20 servings
Preparation time 15 minutes.**

Ingredients:

- ½ lb unsalted butter or ghee

- 1 cup whole grain flour

- 1 cup sugar

- 3 cups water.

Method:

Combine the sugar and water in a saucepan and bring to the boil.

Melt the ghee and add the flour, stirring continuously to lightly toast flour.

Continue stirring the flour and butter mixture while boiling the sugar to make a light syrup.

The butter will separate from the flour, turning a deep golden colour.

Pour the sugar syrup into the flour and butter mixture, stirring rapidly until all water is absorbed.

Keep stirring until the mixture thickens into a firm pudding.

Once completely cooked, the prashad should slide easily from the pan into a bowl.

Cut into individual portions.

Method:

Send letters home asking parents for any donations, giving a list of suggestions, but do state that any donations will be very gratefully received. Include information on where you intend to send your gift boxes.

Some suggestions could be a local homeless shelter, or care home.

Let children decorate the boxes with collage materials before adding the food items, making sure all children have seen the contents. Include a note informing the recipient of the name of your group, to make it a bit more personal before delivering your boxes.

Circle time rhymes: people who help us

Miss Polly

*Miss Polly had a dolly
Who was sick, sick, sick,
So she called for the doctor
To be quick, quick, quick;
The doctor came
With his bag and his hat,
And he knocked at the door
With a rat-a-tat-tat.*

*He looked at the dolly
And he shook his head,
And he said "Miss Polly,
Put her straight to bed."
He wrote out a paper
For a pill, pill, pill,
"I'll be back in the morning
With my bill, bill, bill."*

Dr Foster

*Doctor Foster
Went to Gloucester
In a shower of rain.
He stepped in a puddle
Right up to his middle
And never went there again!*

Five little firemen

*5 little firemen standing in a row
1 2 3 4 5 let's go!
Jump on the engine with a shout
As quick as a wink the fire is out!*

Pat a cake, Pat a cake

Pat a cake, Pat a cake, baker's man
Bake me a cake as fast as you can;
Pat it and prick it and mark it with 'B',
And put in the oven for Baby and me.

Links to learning – EYFS Development Matters

Although the activities in this chapter would fit into many areas of development, I think they may be best suited to Communication and Language.

There is a strong travel theme running through many of the activities which provide so many opportunities for opening up lots of conversations on topics such as; how and why we travel, and special places we have travelled to.

(Looking specifically at the 40-60+ months age group.)

Communication and Language – Understanding

A Unique Child

Responds to instructions involving a two-part sequence.

Understands humour, e.g. nonsense rhymes, jokes.

Able to follow a story without pictures or props.

Listens and responds to ideas expressed by others in conversation or discussion.

Early Learning Goal

Children follow instructions involving several ideas or actions.

They answer 'how' and 'why' questions about their experiences and in response to stories or events.

Communication and Language – Listening and Attention

A Unique Child

Maintains attention, concentrates and sits quietly during appropriate activity.

Two-channelled attention – can listen and do for short span.

Early Learning Goal

Children listen attentively in a range of situations. They listen to stories, accurately anticipating key events and respond to what they hear with relevant comments, questions or actions.

They give their attention to what others say and respond appropriately, while engaged in another activity.

Communication and Language – Speaking

A Unique Child

Extends vocabulary, especially by grouping and naming, exploring the meaning and sounds of new words.

Uses language to imagine and recreate roles and experiences in play situations.

Links statements and sticks to a main theme or intention.

Uses talk to organise, sequence and clarify thinking, ideas, feelings and events.

Introduces a storyline or narrative into their play.

Early Learning Goal

Children express themselves effectively, showing awareness of listeners' needs.

They use past, present and future forms accurately when talking about events that have happened or are to happen in the future.

They develop their own narratives and explanations by connecting ideas or events.

December: Christmas around the world

Christmas is a religious festival celebrated by Christians across the world, generally on 25th December.

Its name derives from the old English word for 'Christ's Mass' and is a celebration of the birth of Jesus Christ, although no-one actually knows when Jesus was born–there's no mention in the **Bible**. It is now believed that Jesus was born sometime between 7BC and 4BC.

Christmas day brings to an end the season of Advent, and begins the twelve days of Christmastide.

Christmas is now a civil holiday in many nations and is celebrated by an increasing number of non-Christians wishing to take part in the celebrations, as a cultural festival.

There are many traditions associated with Christmas, many with no religious significance. **Santa Claus**, or **Father Christmas**, has to be the favourite tradition among children, with families each having their own family traditions concerning where Santa leaves his presents and at which time they get opened. Santa is a common tradition across the world, but there are many variations concerning his appearance and the part he plays in Christmas. The following are just a few examples.

Santa in Belgium

There are two different Santa Claus figures in Belgium, **St. Niklaas** and **Père Noël**. Pere Noel visits children who speak the Walloon language – a regional French dialect originating in Wallonia; a southern region of Belgium. In fact, he visits them twice, first on December 4th to find out which children have been good – or not, and again on December 6th , with gifts for all the good children, but if children have not been too good they are left twigs which he traditionally puts either in their shoes or in a small basket left inside the doorway. **Père Noël** has a companion; **Père Fouettard**, whose chief job is to find out which children have been behaving well.

In the Dutch speaking or 'Flemish' part of Belgium children are visited by St Niklaas on 6th December (Feast of St. Nicholas), which is St. Nicholas' birthday, and he brings gifts to all the children. The feast of St Nicholas is also observed as a religious occasion, and is observed with services in churches. Special cakes are baked as a special treat and it's a time for family gatherings

Santa in America

Christmas celebrations vary greatly between regions in America due to the variety of nationalities having settled there. But Santa is a popular tradition across America.

The traditional modern day Santa we know today actually derived, to a large extent, from the imaginations of the Coca Cola advertisers. Taking inspiration from the famous 1822 poem, 'Twas the Night Before Christmas' by Clement Clark Moore, artist Haddon Sundblom, depicted Santa as described by Moore as part of a coca cola advertising campaign and his design became the blueprint for the well-known chubby, bearded Santa with the red suit and sack of toys.

Early European settlers brought many of their own traditions to the United States. In Hawaii for example, Christmas begins with the arrival of the Christmas Tree Ship, which is a ship not only bringing lots of special Christmas fare, but Santa himself. In California, Santa sweeps in on his surf board.

The traditional American Christmas dinner is roast turkey, followed by Christmas pudding and brandy sauce or pumpkin pie, as well as mince pies. Traditionally, Christmas day begins with Midnight Mass, and later the majority of Americans exchange gifts with family and friends. American homes are often decorated with holly, mistletoe and greenery and most homes have a Christmas tree decorated with little lights, tinsel, strings of popcorn, candy canes and coloured baubles.

Santa in Mexico

In Mexico, Christmas celebrations start December 12th and end January 6th, with children receiving their main presents on January 6th (Epiphany). In Mexico this is known as '**El Dia de los Reyes**' (the day of The Three Kings) and it is the three kings who leave the gifts for many children.

There is also a special cake eaten at this time of year called 'Rosca de Reyes' (Three Kings Cake) in which a small figure of Baby Jesus is hidden. Whoever is lucky enough to find the figure in their slice of cake is the 'Godparent' of Jesus for a year. Presents can also be brought by '**El Niñito Dios**' (baby Jesus) or Santa Claus.

Santa in Slovenia

In Slovenia, Saint Nicholas (Miklavz) brings small gifts for children on the eve of December 6th, **Bozicek** (Christmas Man) brings gifts on the eve of December 25th and **Dedek Mraz** (Grandfather Frost) brings his gifts on December 31st which are opened on New Year's Day.

Santa in Hungary

In Hungary, Saint Nicolaus (Mikulas) arrives on the night of December 5th, with children finding their gifts the next morning, placed in their shoes.

He brings good children little bags of sweets and small gifts, but naughty ones receive birch twigs, an onion, or something similar. The shoes however, usually contain both nice and less desirable gifts, representing the fact that no child is entirely good or bad. Sometimes Saint Nicolaus is accompanied by 'Krampusz', a devilish figure who counteracts Saint Nicolaus' good spirit.

On Christmas Eve, 'Little Jesus' or angels visit homes, bringing children sweets and gifts and magically decorating Christmas trees.

Leaving presents for Santa

Although it is customary in America and Canada to leave Santa milk and cookies, children in Britain and Australia often leave something a bit stronger, such as a beer or a glass of sherry to keep him going on his long journey, plus, if he's lucky, a mince pie.

In Norway and Sweden Santa gets rice porridge, while in Ireland it is popular to leave a Guinness with Santa's mince pie.

Ask children in your group about some of the things they will be doing over the Christmas holidays. Who leaves a carrot for Rudolf? Even children whose families don't celebrate Christmas will be going somewhere at some point over the holidays, so everyone can join in.

Make a Santa's Workshop home corner

Always popular, the play, or home corner, is brilliant for building both imagination and social skills. At this time of year, why not make it extra special by turning it into a simple Santa's workshop. If you don't already have a home corner you can easily set one up, just a table and a couple of chairs is all you really need – it's all in the detail. For a Santa's workshop include a little Christmas tree if you have one, some really inexpensive wrapping paper, sticky tape and toys to wrap, plus play carpentry tools and some junk modelling supplies – so the elves can construct something amazing!

If the play corner is getting a bit over-crowded, you could consider time-tabling it, so all children get a chance to play. Also, let children experiment with the wrapping and construction materials without encouraging them to make a neat job, or something recognisable, as it's all about fun, besides, trial and error is the best way to learn the tricky art of construction.

A Christmas play

This simple narrated storyline makes for a great little Christmas play. I've used it many times with my youngest groups and it always proves really popular with both the audience, and the children taking part.

Try borrowing a couple of slightly older children to play the parts of Mrs Mabbs and the landlord – they'll really like to help, and younger children love working with older ones.

If older children are to take part they might like to speak the dialogue. If so, simply transfer their lines from the narration.

Have a few practice sessions so children get used to standing really still and acting out their parts.

Also, explain what is meant by the term 'landlord'.

Essential resources

- Costumes to make children look like toys. Improvise here; party dresses/tutus for dolls, cowboy hats, action man outfits etc. See what children have at home. You can use face paints to make nice pink dolly cheeks and teddy bear noses

- Toy broom or mop, chair, and handkerchief or tissue for Mrs Mabbs.

- Xylophone or something similar to make the clock's chimes.

- Magical music, something like, 'Aquarium' from 'The Carnival of the Animals' by Saint-Saëns.

- Cleaning and mending props for the toys; dusters, dustpans and brushes, play tools etc.

Mrs Mabbs' Toyshop

Narrator: Welcome to our Christmas assembly. Today we are going to perform our special Christmas play – I hope you all enjoy it. Our play is called; Mrs Mabb's Toyshop.

Mrs Mabbs is sweeping the floor of her little toy shop. She stops now and then to rub her back and shake her head. Other children dressed as toys are standing completely still behind her in their poses.

It was the evening of Christmas Eve, and Mrs Mabbs, who was very old, was trying to sweep the floor of the little toy shop where she had lived for many years. Poor Mrs Mabbs was not very strong. Her back was aching and she was quite shaky on her feet, so she wasn't able to make a very good job of keeping the shop clean and tidy, even though she did try very hard to keep it nice. Suddenly, there was a knock at the door.

Someone makes a knocking sound.

Mrs Mabbs opened the door, and in walked Mr Jones, the landlord, who owned the shop.

The landlord walks in.

"Good evening Mrs Mabbs," he said. "I have come to inspect the shop and make sure you are looking after it as well as you should be."

The landlord starts to inspect the toys, running his hand over a couple of the children's head's, rubbing his hands together in disgust at the dust and wags his finger at Mrs Mabbs in disapproval.

He said, "I'm afraid, Mrs Mabbs, that the shop just isn't clean enough and there are lots of repairs that need taking care of. I'm afraid you are just too old and weak to look after the shop any longer. I think it would be better if you went to live somewhere else, then I could get this shop tidied up so someone else could live here and take care of the toy shop for me".

Mrs Mabbs dabs her eyes with her handkerchief.

Mrs Mabbs was so upset she started to cry a little bit and dabbed her eyes with her handkerchief. She said," Please Mr Jones, don't make me live somewhere else. I love this little toy shop. I promise to work really hard to get it really clean and mended". "I'm not sure about that," said Mr Jones. "But seeing as it's Christmas time, I will give you a chance to get the shop tidied up. You have until first thing tomorrow morning – Christmas Day, to get this shop completely clean and mended. If you do and I come back tomorrow to find everything is done as it should be – you can stay, but if not – you will have to leave I'm afraid." And with that he walked out the door.

The landlord walks out of the door and Mrs Mabbs sits down sadly in a chair with her head in her hands.

Mrs Mabbs was so sad. She knew she wouldn't be able to get the shop clean and mended by morning and didn't know what to do. She had one last look at all the toys in the shop, then went to bed.

Mrs Mabbs has a little look at the toys then walks off shaking her head.

As Mrs Mabbs slept, the clock chimed twelve times.

Someone makes the twelve chimes on a xylophone.

It was now Christmas Morning – a time when magic can happen!

Play music as all toys very slowly start to stretch. They start to move about, cleaning and repairing the shop with their cleaning props and tools (which are placed at the side of the performing space) until you signal for them to go back to their places, once again keeping completely still as you gradually fade the music out.

When Mrs Mabbs woke up she felt very sad. She knew she would have to leave the toy shop because she hadn't been able to do the cleaning or repairs. But as she walked into the shop, she couldn't believe her eyes.

Mrs Mabbs walks into the shop yawning and stretching, then looks astounded as she sees everything has been done – shaking her head and rubbing her eyes in disbelief.

The shop was as clean and good as new. All the cleaning and repairs had been taken care of. But who could have done it? Mrs Mabbs shook her head and rubbed her eyes in disbelief. Just then there came a knock at the door.

Someone makes a knocking sound.

It was Mr. Jones, the Landlord. He was back to inspect the shop.

The landlord walks in and again inspects the shop and toys.

He said: "Mrs Mabbs, I must say, you have done a splendid job. Yes everything seems to be taken care of here. There isn't any reason for you to leave now, and I am happy for you to carry on living here."

Mrs Mabbs looks very happy as the landlord turns and leaves, calling, "Merry Christmas Mrs Mabbs." Mrs Mabbs replies, "Merry Christmas Mr Jones."

Mrs Mabbs stood looking at the lovely clean shop, wondering who on earth could have cleaned and mended everything while she was asleep.

Mrs Mabbs says: "It must have been Christmas magic!". As she walks off stage, shaking her head in disbelief. After she has left, toys turn to each other and giggle.

That is the end of the story of Mrs Mabbs toyshop.

We hope you enjoyed it and we'd like to wish you all a Very Merry Christmas!

All children take a bow.

End with a chorus of 'We wish you a Merry Christmas'.

- The **candle** symbolises Jesus, the light of the world.

- The **red ribbon** represents the love and blood of Christ.

- The **sweets** and fruit are symbols of God's creations.

Have a go at making your own Christingles, they look lovely, smell lovely and make a really nice hand-made Christmas gift for children to give to a family member.

Make it!

Make a Christingle

You will need (per Christingle):

- 1 orange

- 1 small candle

- 1 piece of foil about 3 inches square – to catch wax drips

- A length of red ribbon or red sticky tape

- 4 cocktail sticks

- An assortment of dried fruit and small sweets, such as dolly mixtures, jelly tots, sultanas and raisins.

Method:

Fasten the length of red ribbon or tape around the middle of the orange.

Cut a small cross in the top of the orange and lay the square of foil on top.

Place the candle on top of the foil and wedge into the orange securely.

Stick the four cocktail sticks, evenly spaced, around the orange and carefully push little sweets and dried fruits onto sticks.

The Christingle service

The word Christingle means 'Christ Light' and celebrates the light of Jesus coming into the world. Lots of churches hold Christingle services around Christmas time. The custom of giving out candles in these services originates from the Moravian Church in Germany in 1747, but didn't make an appearance in the English Anglican church until around 1968.

There is a story relating to the Christingle custom, which is that there were once three children who although very poor, wanted to give a gift to Jesus like all the other children were going to do at church. The only nice thing they could find was an orange, so they decided to use it as their gift. As the top of the orange had gone a bit green, they cut it off and the eldest child placed a candle in the hole. The youngest child tied her best red ribbon around the orange, fastening it in place with toothpicks, and the youngest child thought it would be nice to put some little pieces of dried fruit on the ends of the sticks, which they did. The children took their orange to church for the Christmas mass, where the other children sneered at their little gift. The priest though, took their gift and showed it as an example of a true understanding of the meaning of Christmas.

Links to learning – EYFS Development Matters

There is a lot of storytelling going on in this chapter, plus lots of dramatic and imaginative play.

Activities cover development points in the area of Expressive Arts and Design as below.

(Looking specifically at the 40-60+ months age group.)

Symbolism of the Christingle

- The **orange** represents the world.

Expressive Arts and Design – Being Imaginative

A Unique Child

Create simple representations of events, people and objects.

Initiates new combinations of movement and gesture in order to express and respond to feelings, ideas and experiences.

Chooses particular colours to use for a purpose.

Introduces a storyline or narrative into their play.

Plays alongside other children who are engaged in the same theme.

Plays cooperatively as part of a group to develop and act out a narrative.

Early Learning Goal

Children use what they have learnt about media and materials in original ways, thinking about uses and purposes.

They represent their own ideas, thoughts and feelings through design and technology, art, music, dance, role play and stories.

The following areas of learning are also covered here,

Understanding the World – The World

A Unique Child

Looks closely at similarities, differences, patterns and change.

Early Learning Goal

Children know about similarities and differences in relation to places, objects, materials and living things.

They talk about the features of their own immediate environment and how environments might vary from one another.

Setting examples of religious and cultural celebrations

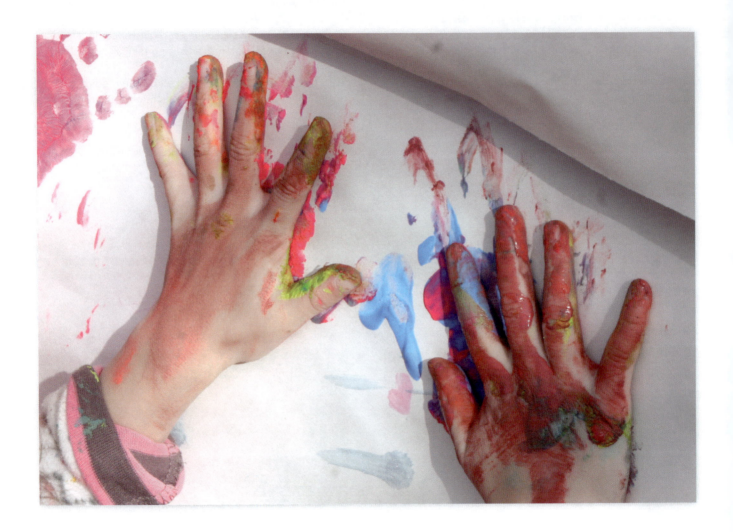

The following examples show the approach that two successful pre-schools have taken in introducing the subject of faiths, cultures and festivals to their pre-school children.

Handsworth Pre-School, North East London

Handsworth Pre-School, London, is an OFSTED registered and PSLA accredited pre-school group which has been running for over twenty five years and caters for children

from two to five years. Here (during a session celebrating the Holi festival) pre-school leader Kitty West, shares her ideas on teaching the subject of faiths and cultures in a pre-school environment.

"The subject of faiths and festivals is not directly taught, but introduced through play and activities.

For example, the Japanese Doll Festival was talked about during circle time and simple origami activities were organised to celebrate the occasion.

At Christmas the children perform a nativity play and sing 'Away in a Manger', although, to be honest, most of the time we find they prefer 'Jingle Bells'. Of course, we also have a Christmas party and organise lots of Christmassy craft activities for the weeks leading up to Christmas.

We always try to mark festivals and customs relating to any children attending our pre-school – to make them feel part of the group. For instance, we celebrated the Japanese Doll Festival primarily because we have two Japanese twins in our group.

We make sure we cover the early year's foundation stage recommendations throughout our planning, but our objective will always be, learning through play.

As our group is run from a church hall, we're not allowed to display any art work or posters on the walls, so we tend to put our art work on big display boards in the hallway for parents and carers to see when they come to collect their children. Today's big group artwork; a rainbow coloured paint and glitter poster (part of their Holi Festival celebration) will be put up for display so parents can see some of what we have been doing today, and also, so children can proudly show their work. Other Holi activities offered today have included:

- Marble rolling using fluorescent paint and black paper

- Multi-coloured crêpe paper streamers for free-play

- Colourful foods at snack time.

Other general activities organised to tie-in with customs and festivals include:

- Stories and rhymes associated with the custom or festival

- Themed craft activities and colouring activity sheets

- Traditional foods."

Charlton Family Centre, South East London

Charlton Family Centre, London, was set up as a project on the Cherry Orchard Estate in 1999, to meet the needs of local families with children under the age of five years. The group is managed by the Pre-school Learning Alliance Greenwich Sub-committee, and operates from a converted building on the estate.

Mona Naqvi is manager of Charlton Family Centre and shares her thoughts on introducing the subject of faiths and festivals to pre-school children.

"Religious occasions are celebrated throughout the year at Charlton Family Centre, but keeping in mind that they should reflect the religious beliefs of the families and staff in the setting. Other religious days are acknowledged by reading a book about it or setting up an area of interest for the children in the rooms.

When a child starts attending the family centre one of the questions in the registration form asks about the child's faith, some parents/carers choose not to fill it in but that is their decision and not questioned by the setting. We then ask parents to complete an Initial Child Profile form for their child, so we can understand the needs and interests of the child from the parent/carer perspective, and ask them about any significant celebrations or festivals celebrated by the family, besides birthdays.

All this information is collated so that the key workers can ensure that all religious and cultural festivals of significance to the families are celebrated in the centre.

At the beginning of the year, a calendar of the year's cultural and religious festivals is printed and dates marked in diaries to ensure no festival is missed.

Nearer the time of the celebration, families are consulted about how to celebrate the festival correctly and if they are able to contribute their time to talk about the festival or bring some artefacts and books in for display. If it is a less well-known festival, a display will be arranged in the hallway to increase awareness amongst all families attending the setting.

It is surprising how acknowledging a family's cultural and religious background brings out discussion and enthusiasm in the most reluctant of individuals."

Easter at Charlton Family Centre

"Easter and Christmas are the two main festivals celebrated at Charlton Family Centre. We start the Easter celebrations by fund raising for our party. Normally a raffle is organised with families and staff contributing Easter Eggs and soft toys for the raffle.

Before organising any major celebrations, staff consult parents on what sort of celebration they would like to take part in this year.

This year families decided that we should take the children for an outing to Danson Park, for an egg hunt, followed by a picnic and games like Tug of war and an egg & spoon race to involve the parents, children and staff together.

Two weeks before the Easter party the staff encouraged parents to make and decorate an Easter bonnet with their child. These Easter bonnets were kept at the family centre until the day of the party, and children made Easter Egg chocolate nests and cards to take away with them too.

Staff do take this opportunity to explain the religious significance of the celebration to children either through books, puppets or displays, with special consideration always given to children whose parents might not be keen on their children joining in certain religious celebrations. These children can join in when making cards or chocolate nests, but the staff do not talk about the reason behind making them or add wording to the card. If possible children are offered alternative sessions to compensate for sessions they might miss because of these celebrations.

On the day of the Easter party this year, the children and their families joined together in an Easter egg hunt in the garden, followed by an Easter bonnet parade around the housing estate singing songs and playing music.

The children and their families including younger siblings then ate party food, before they went home with a small Easter egg as a gift from the family centre.

In the past we have had Easter egg hunts with a twist where families were encouraged to look for clues around the family centre and garden to find Easter eggs and chicks."

Christmas at Charlton Family Centre

"It has been a year of celebration and fun for our children and families, with Christmas bringing it to an amazing finale.

This year the children have taken part in a Christmas disco, which was an opportunity for young and old to polish their disco moves before Christmas. It was a well-attended affair with a snack buffet for all to enjoy and Santa paying a visit while on his travels to hand out sweets to the children.

We also created a Winter wonderland grotto, giving children the chance to tell Santa what they wanted for Christmas and take a ride on his magical sleigh.

Our carol singing celebrations are always well attended with families joining in with their children to sing and eat mince pies.

Our children have been practising hard for their Christmas performances, with older children performing a play and younger children singing songs to their families.

The Christmas party brings the season of celebration to a close with a roast lunch and theatre entertainment in the afternoon."

Children's name board

Charlton Family Centre have included a 'children's name board' in their setting, which is, I think, a lovely, simple way of celebrating individualism and getting parents involved in the group in a small and simple way. It's also great if like me, you're just interested in the reasons why parents choose the names the do.

Parents have contributed short hand-written notes detailing the reasons for choosing their children's names and these have been pinned to the board.

The board is headed as follows:

'Sunshine room is made up of unique and interesting individuals. Please take the time to read why we are so special'

Samples of parent's contributions:

Abdullah

'From the Arabic name meaning 'Servant of Allah'. He is a great provider of love and understanding. Always strives for greatness. Someone that can be relied upon. He is truly special.

Nishan

Nishan means 'prize'. The reason I named her Nishan is because she is my first daughter and it means a world of pride to me.

Rafi and Violet

Rafi is named after his Pakistani grandfather and the meaning of Rafi is 'friend'. Violet is named after her Scottish great grandmother and the meaning is 'fragrant flower'.

Religious places and practices – at a glance

Jewish faith

- A Jewish place of worship is called a **synagogue**, where men and women usually sit separately.

- Worship usually takes place in **Hebrew** and men are required to cover their heads.

- The Jewish spiritual leaders are called **rabbis** and unlike leaders of many other faiths, a rabbi is not a priest and possesses no special religious status.

- The Jewish religious text is the **Tanakh** or Hebrew Bible.

- The **Star of David** is a well-known symbol of Judaism.

Christian faith

- A Christian place of worship is called a **church**. Christian spiritual leaders are called **priests** or **ministers** or **vicars** (depending on denomination of the church).

- Christianity is the world's most widely followed religion – roughly 2.2 billion followers worldwide.

- Christians follow the teachings of **Jesus Christ** – a Jew, born roughly 2000 years ago in the Palestinian city of Bethlehem, whom Christians believe is God's son.

- Each year Christians celebrate Jesus' birth at **Christmas** and his death and resurrection at **Easter**.

- Christians worship God through music, readings from scripture, prayers, sermons and holy ceremonies, following the word of the Christian holy book – **The Bible**.

- The Bible is divided into two sections – **The Old** and **New Testaments**. (Parts of the Old Testament are also sacred to those of the Muslim and Jewish faith.)

- Christians believe that there is only one God, and that he is **The Father, The Son and The Holy Spirit**, collectively known as The Trinity. These three divine 'natures' are distinct, but are also one.

Hindu faith

- A Hindu building of communal worship is called a **mandir** (Hindu Temple) These temples are dedicated to different Gods. Outside India, people generally meet at the mandir at the weekend.

- Hindus worship by repeating the names of their favourite Gods, Goddesses, and the mantras. Water, fruit, flowers and incense are also used as offerings to the Gods.

- Many Hindus also worship at home where they have a shrine, which can be represented by anything from a room, to a small altar or simply pictures of statues.

Offerings are made to a sacred statue of a god or goddess known as a murti.

Muslim faith

- A Muslim place of communal worship is called a **mosque** and services are held here every day, with the most important service being held every Friday at noon – a special day for prayer.

- Women and men worship in separate areas within the mosque.

- Every mosque has a Quibla Wall, which is the wall facing Makkah (Mecca); the holiest city in the Islamic religion.

- Mosques also contain a place to wash (wudu). Muslims wash their hands, mouth, throat, nose, ears, arms up to the elbow and feet. This symbolises spiritual cleansing and purity in readiness for coming before God.

- Mosques usually have a domed roof and a tall tower called a minaret. A man known as a muezzin enters the minaret and calls Muslims to prayer, although this is not permitted in Britain – some Islamic communities now broadcast the call to prayer by means of radio waves to be picked up by Muslims in their homes or places of work.

- There is very little furniture in a mosque as Muslims pray on prayer mats, and there are no statues or pictures, but there are decorations of patterns and words from the Islamic holy book (**Qur'an**).

- Shoes are removed before entering a mosque to keep it clean for prayer.

Sikh faith

- A Sikh place of worship is called the **gurdwara** (Gateway to the Guru), but Sikhs also worship at home.

- All Gurdwaras contain:

  ○ The **Guru Granth Sahib** (Sikh scripture)

  ○ The Langar (Community Kitchen), where food is prepared by all members of the Gurdwara to demonstrate a belief in equality of all, irrespective of caste, creed, religion, sex or race.

  ○ The Nishan Sahib – a yellow (saffron) triangular flag bearing the Sikh symbol (Khanda) which flies from every Gurdwara. In the Sikh tradition 'Nishan Sahib' means 'the holy flag' or 'exalted ensign'.

○ Four Doors – The **gurdwara** usually has four doors to show it is open to all.

Buddhist faith

● Buddhists worship at home or in a temple, often barefoot sitting on the floor, facing an image of **Buddha**. It is very important that Buddhists have their feet pointing away from Buddha (a show of respect).

● Buddhists chant and listen to monks chanting from religious texts, meditate, read from holy books and take part in prayer sessions as part of their worship.

● Many Buddhists will have a shrine at home containing a statue of Buddha, candles and an incense burner.

● Buddhist temples are designed in many shapes, but all contain a statue or image of Buddha.

● Buddhist worship is called Puja. Buddhists chant to demonstrate love and devotion to Buddha, as well as making offerings of flowers, candles, pure water and incense.

● Every month, usually on days when there is a full moon, many Buddhists go to temples to worship. Full moon days are of special religious significance to Buddhists as certain important events in the life of Buddha took place on full moon days.

Jehovah's Witness faith

● Jehovah's Witnesses worship and study their religion at Kingdom Halls, which contain no religious symbols and are typically functional in design and character. Witnesses attend meetings where they study Watch Tower Society literature and the Bible, and which are scheduled by congregation elders.

● Congregations meet for two sessions each week and are opened and closed with Kingdom Songs (hymns) and prayers.

● The most important religious event for Jehovah's Witnesses is the commemoration of the Lord's Evening Meal; in memory of Christ's Death. This takes place on the date of the Jewish Passover – falling in March or April in the Gregorian (Western) calendar.

The month-by-month calendar on page 3 of this book could be used to include such dates as: school outings, important dates for your local community, national events and any religious or cultural festivals you wish to plan for.

Appendix: Simple warm-up games

These are simple, fun games that get everyone fired up and ready for some drama fun. Young children like to play games they know and will often ask for their favourites. Once children are familiar with a few games, let them take turns to pick one, and they'll soon start to really look forward to this part of the lesson, which is great for getting children all playing together.

Walking the tightrope

Although this is as simple as can be, it is a great favourite with this age group.

Simply draw a chalk line down the centre of the room as an imaginary tightrope for children to walk along, being as careful as they can not to fall off. Make the line a bit curvy to make it more interesting, and space children out a bit to stop them getting too bunched up.

In my pudding pot

A really simple game, but great for firing-up imaginations at the beginning of a session.

Children sit in a circle, taking turns to come into the middle to stir their pretend pudding mixture while saying, 'In my pudding pot I'm putting a…' adding the name of something they can stir into their pudding mixture, which can be anything at all; a banana or an elephant, for example. Make your own variations such as, in my magic witches' pot, or a seasonal Christmas pudding pot.

Animal moves

Start by letting children move around the room pretending to be any animal they like, but give a few suggestions for anyone stuck for an idea. Next, tell children to become specific animals as you call them out – animal sounds included. Some good ones to use are:

- Monkey
- Crocodile
- Lion

- Frog
- Dog
- Snake
- Owl
- Mouse.

Follow this by asking children to now imagine they are:

- A monkey peeling and eating a banana
- A cat creeping up and pouncing on a mouse
- A little mouse peeping out of its hole, then scurrying out to look for some cheese, but being very frightened that the cat might catch him.

Finish by asking children to make the following movements – asking for suggestions to which animals would make them:

- Slither
- Gallop
- Swim
- Hop
- Pounce
- Fly
- Scurry
- Jump.

Emotions

Ask children to walk around the room imagining they are feeling the following emotions:

- Happy

- Sad

- Excited

- Frightened.

Next give the following scenarios and have children respond with an appropriate emotion:

- You have just won a million pounds

- You have trodden in a big muddy puddle

- You are about to go on a scary fairground ride

- You have just accidently broken your favourite toy

- Your mum has given you a lovely ice cream … Oh No! You've dropped it.

Eating mime

An idea for a mini activity which acts as a good introduction to role play and mime is the eating mime.

For this activity children simply sit quietly and are told to imagine they are eating or drinking various nice and nasty foods; showing through facial expressions how these make them feel (sound effects permitted). Start off by demonstrating yourself.

Ideas of things to eat could include:

- A very hot and spicy burger

- A lemon

- Favourite chocolate bar

- A freezing cold drink

- A drink that is too hot

- Horrible medicine

- Long spaghetti

- Very sticky toffee

- A slug or snail.

Magical balloon ride

An activity involving lots of running about, jumping and stretching – plus, a fair bit of imagination.

Essential resources:

- A few chairs.

Method:

The first thing to do is section off a bit of your space using chairs, or something similar. This area will be the hot air balloon. You can add a couple of cushions or a blanket if you like, as the floor will become the balloon's basket.

Next, tell children that today they are going on a make believe balloon ride to all sorts of exciting places, so climb aboard and we'll see where we float off to!

Once everyone is sitting in the balloon, say: 'I'm just going to untie the big rope that's holding the balloon down – so get ready to float away everyone!' And pretend to untie the rope.

Make the journey fun by saying things like; 'It's getting very windy now – so hold on tight! Or, Oh no! It's starting to rain – all hide under the blanket, quick!

Next, tell children the balloon is floating back down, but where is it landing? Say: 'Hold on tight everyone and get ready for a big bump 1…2…3… bump! And we've landed at … The seaside! Hooray! See if you can find some buckets and spades and sun cream in the basket, and everyone jump out and play on the beach'. If children get stuck with the imaginary play, help them along with some ideas for things to do on the beach – having a picnic, building sandcastles, paddling in the sea, eating an ice cream, being chased by a crab… Then it's everyone back in the balloon ready to take off for the next adventure.

Some ideas for locations to visit in your balloon could be:

- The North Pole – good for a snowball fight

- A fun-fair – you could set up a mini activity for this, something like trying to throw a beanbag into a bucket

- A magical land where everything is made of sweets.

To end the activity, everyone travels back home and waves goodbye to the balloon as it floats away, to return again another day.

End of session rhyme

End a drama session with a quick and simple action rhyme. Try using the same one every time – children love the familiarity. The following is a favourite of mine.

Think of a giant – stretch as tall as you can

Think of a mouse – make yourself as small as you can

Think of a palace – Use arms to make a tall palace shape

Think of a house – Bring arms down to make a smaller building

Think of an eagle – Flap arms like big wings

Think of a wren – Flap arms like little wings

Think of a wrist watch – Point to wrist

Think of Big Ben – Clasp hands and swing arms like a pendulum, making three 'bongs'.

A few more ideas:

The following old favourites all make good warm-up games:

- The farmer's in his den

- Here we go round the mulberry bush

- The grand old Duke of York

- The Hokey Cokey

- Ring a Ring o' Roses

- What's the time Mr Wolf?

- Simon says…

- Musical statues

- Musical bumps

- Sleeping Lions – a really good calm-down game.

Acknowledgements

I would like to thank:

Danielle Hart (BA hons in education, MA in special educational needs and SpLD) for all her help throughout, Joy Gailer, (LGSM) (in my opinion the world's best drama teacher), Kitty West and Mona Naqvi – inspirational early years practitioners.

I would like to thank Lucie Carlier for taking the lovely photos.

Thank you to the settings, practitioners and parents of Handsworth Pre-school and Charlton Family Centre, for allowing me to use their celebration examples and pictures for this book.

I hope this book will be useful to anyone wishing to explore the subject of faiths and festivals with young children – have fun!

All children pictured throughout this book are shown to represent children playing and learning in a multi-cultural environment. They are not shown as individually representing any specific religion. If their inclusion appears to indicate a connection with a particular religious group, this is purely unintentional.

Notes